5G and Cloud

5G and Cloud

Synergy Transforms Telecommunications

RAFEAL MECHLORE

WSM Publisher

CONTENTS

INDEX

INTRODUCTION

If someone had told you in the early 2000s that your smartphone would become a versatile digital companion, capable of linking you to people and information around the globe at rates that were once considered to be unimaginable, you might have brushed it off as science fiction. But today, that is exactly what your smartphone is capable of doing. However, if we fast forward to the present, we can see that the reality is much more astounding than the most fantastic dreams of that era. This unprecedented transition is being led by the convergence of 5G and cloud technologies, which is changing the telecoms industry in ways that were previously inconceivable.

This book, titled "5G and Cloud Synergy Transforms Telecommunications," investigates the deep impact of this synergy by digging into the technical, practical, and societal components of this dynamic cooperation. The book's title comes from the fact that this synergy is transforming the field of telecommunications. In the following two thousand words, we are going to embark on a journey through the development of telecommunications, the complexities of 5G technology, the power of cloud computing, and how the interplay between 5G and the cloud is reshaping the very fabric of our connected world. This journey will take us through the evolution of telecommunications, the intricacies of 5G technology, the power of cloud computing, and more.

The Development of the Communications Industry

It is necessary to go back to the beginning of the field of telecommunications in order to fully comprehend the significance of the synergy between 5G and the cloud. From smoke signals and carrier pigeons to the advent of the telegraph in the 19th century, the idea of transferring information over large distances has a history that spans thousands of years. The telegraph was the first successful method of doing so. It was the invention of the telegraph that paved the way for global communication by making it possible for messages to be transmitted across continents at a rate that had never been seen before.

The technology used for communications have progressed over time. The invention of the telephone democratized voice communication and made it possible for people to interact with one another in real time, regardless of the physical distance that separated them. The following development of digital networks and the internet contributed significantly to the continued expansion of the capabilities of the telecommunications industry.

The Coming of Age of 3G and 4G

The introduction of 3G (third-generation) and later 4G (fourth-generation) networks at the beginning of the 21st century was an important turning point in the field of telecommunications. This was a turning point that signified a significant turning point in the field.

These innovations completely altered the ways in which we interact with mobile devices. They pioneered the development of better data transmission speeds, mobile internet access, and an ecosystem of applications that eventually got ingrained in our routines. The age of smartphones had officially arrived.

Nevertheless, despite the potential of 4G, there remained constraints that prevented the seamless integration of technology into a variety of facets of daily life. Because of the increasing demand for high-definition video streaming, augmented reality applications, and the Internet of Things (IoT), connectivity problems, delay in data transfer, and the requirement for even faster rates became apparent.

The Urgent Need for 5G and Collaboration in the Cloud

It became more and more obvious that an entirely new generation of wireless technology was required. These issues can be overcome with the implementation of 5G, which is the fifth generation of wireless technology. It is not only an incremental upgrade but rather a leap into the future, promising to deliver data speeds that are orders of magnitude faster than its predecessors. This is not a simple improvement but rather a leap into the future. 5G is going to make it possible for us to live and work in new ways because it will have data transfer rates of up to 20 gigabits per second and latency of only one millisecond.

The possibilities of 5G are astounding, but with those capabilities come a complexity and set of requirements that are higher than those required by past generations of telecommunications technologies. We require a dependable and adaptable infrastructure in order to make the most of the promise offered by 5G. The cloud becomes relevant at this point in the game.

The Crucial Function that Connectivity Plays in Today's Society

It is essential that, as we move forward with our investigation of the synergy between 5G and the cloud, we keep in mind the key place that connectivity holds in today's society. Our lives have become increasingly reliant on our capacity for frictionless communication, rapid information access, and the exchange of experiences with those located over great distances. The field of telecommunications is more than just a technological one; it is also a social force that influences how we live, work, and communicate with one another.

In this day and age, when corporations compete on a worldwide scale, medical professionals are able to remotely monitor their patients, and education has expanded beyond the bounds of the traditional classroom, it is impossible to emphasize the significance of having dependable and high-speed connections. The foundation of the digital economy is the telecommunications industry, which connects people and gadgets, paves the way for trade, and propels innovation.

The field of telecommunications is in and of itself a fluid and ever-shifting terrain that exerts a significant influence on economies, other fields of industry, and national governments. It is a domain in which new ideas, new policies, and new technologies come together to influence how people all over the world communicate. This book will walk you through this dynamic landscape, shining light on the synergy between 5G and the cloud that is propelling telecommunications into a new era. It will also help you navigate the tremendous opportunities that lie ahead.

As we move further in our trip, we will investigate the complexities of 5G technology, gain an understanding of the power of cloud computing, look into the confluence of these two technologies, and investigate the revolutionary influence that these technologies will have on many businesses, as well as on overall society. This book intends to be an all-encompassing resource that will equip you with the information and understanding you require to successfully traverse the rapidly advancing world of 5G and cloud synergy in the field of telecommunications. Therefore, let's get started on this voyage of discovery, and together, let's investigate how 5G and cloud synergy are actually reshaping the field of telecommunications in ways that only a few short years ago were nothing more than pipe dreams.

1. **Definition and Importance of 5G and Cloud Synergy**

   The symbiotic relationship between fifth-generation (5G) wireless technology and cloud computing has emerged as a critical factor driving innovation and transformation across industries. This is due to the continuously changing landscape of modern technology. Cloud computing increases the potential of 5G by offering a scalable and adaptable infrastructure to accommodate the deluge of data generated by 5G-enabled devices and apps. As 5G revolutionizes communication with its high-speed and low-latency capabilities, cloud computing amplifies the potential of 5G. This powerful synergy between 5G and cloud computing ushers in a new era in the field of telecommunications and will redefine the ways in which we communicate, conduct business, and engage with the world around us.

   Acquiring Knowledge of 5G

   The fifth generation of wireless technology, often known as 5G, marks a paradigm leap in the field of telecommunications. It promises data transfer rates that have never been seen before, improved connectivity, and extremely low latency. In contrast to its predecessors, 5G is not primarily focused on enhancing the experience of consumers. Instead, it seeks to serve as an enabler for a wide variety of applications that span numerous industries, such as healthcare, manufacturing, transportation, and entertainment. 5G provides the framework for the Internet of Things (IoT) and the development of smart, interconnected devices because to its ability to support a vast number of connected devices at the same time. Fostering innovation and propelling society into an era of greater connectedness and seamless integration are two of the benefits that will accrue from the widespread use of this technology, which will serve as the backbone for the expanding digital ecosystem.

The Benefits of Working in the Cloud

In the meantime, cloud computing has emerged as the central pillar of modern data management. Cloud computing provides businesses with scalable and on-demand services that make it possible for them to efficiently store, process, and manage large volumes of data. Cloud services include a variety of solutions, such as Infrastructure as a Service (IaaS), Platform as a Service (PaaS), and Software as a Service (SaaS). These services give businesses the tools they need to improve efficiency, cut costs, and encourage innovation. Cloud computing offers organizations a competitive advantage in a world that is becoming increasingly digital by allowing them to scale their operations without the limits of physical infrastructure. Cloud computing is characterized by its flexibility and agility.

5G and Cloud Computing: A Complementary Relationship

A transformational factor that is altering the landscape of telecommunications is the combination of fifth-generation (5G) wireless networking with cloud computing. This synergy enhances the capabilities of both technologies by capitalizing on their respective strengths. The result is the creation of an all-encompassing ecosystem that gives power to both corporations and individual customers. The lightning-fast speeds of 5G and the strong architecture of the cloud enable businesses to harness the potential of real-time data processing, which in turn enables the development of creative apps and services that were previously unreachable.

Increased Connectivity as well as Velocity

The enhancement of connectivity and speed is one of the primary advantages that comes as a result of the synergy between 5G and cloud computing. Users will have the capacity to experience continuous, uninterrupted connectivity thanks to the unrivaled data transfer speeds made possible by 5G and the cloud's ability to analyze data in real time. This will allow users to access and share information in an instant. This improved connectivity paves the way for new opportunities for businesses, making it possible for them to provide customers with individualized and immersive experiences and facilitating the quick transfer of large data sets, which is essential for a variety of applications including augmented reality, virtual reality, and high-definition video streaming.

Scalability and adaptability go hand in together.

In addition, the combination of 5G wireless networking with cloud computing delivers unrivaled scalability and flexibility, which enables businesses to more easily respond to shifting customer requirements and scale their operations without disruption. An infrastructure that is located on the cloud makes it possible for businesses to increase their resources on demand, allowing them to accommodate abrupt spikes in data traffic without the need to make major expenditures in physical hardware. This scalability, when combined with 5G's capacity to support a large number of connected devices, assures that companies will be able to satisfy the ever-changing requirements of their clientele while retaining the agility necessary to remain competitive in a market that is constantly shifting.

Putting the Internet of Things and Edge Computing to Work

The Internet of Things (IoT) and edge computing capabilities will both benefit greatly from the synergy that exists between fifth-generation wireless (5G) technology and cloud computing. IoT devices will be able to communicate with one another in a seamless manner because to the high bandwidth and low latency offered by 5G. This will enable the development of interconnected systems that will expedite operations, enhance efficiency, and drive innovation across a variety of different industries. Integration of edge computing, which involves processing data closer to the source, further optimizes the performance of Internet of Things devices by lowering latency and boosting real-time decision-making capabilities. Edge computing involves processing data closer to the source than traditional cloud computing. Businesses are able to tap into the full potential of the Internet of Things (IoT) and edge computing when they leverage the cloud for storage and processing power. This ushers in an era of intelligent, networked gadgets that has the potential to alter the way we live and work.

Creating the Conditions for Innovation and Transformation

The synergy between fifth-generation wireless (5G) networks and cloud computing will serve as a driver of innovation and transformation across all sectors of the economy. This cooperation enables businesses to develop and implement cutting-edge technologies and services that drive growth and foster a competitive edge by offering a solid infrastructure for data management and processing. This infrastructure enables organizations to drive growth. The convergence of 5G and cloud computing generates a wave of revolutionary solutions that have the ability to revolutionize whole industries and redefine the way in which people engage with technology. These solutions range from sophisticated analytics and artificial intelligence to immersive virtual experiences and autonomous systems. Moreover, these solutions are fueled by the convergence of 5G and cloud computing.

Increasing Reliability While Maintaining Security

The partnership between fifth-generation (5G) wireless networking and cloud computing not only propels innovation but also improves the safety and dependability of telecommunications networks. Cloud-based security solutions provide sophisticated mechanisms for detecting and preventing threats, thereby protecting data and communications from the risks and vulnerabilities posed by prospective cyber attacks. In addition, the stringent security standards of 5G, in conjunction with the encryption and authentication capabilities of the cloud, guarantee that sensitive information is kept safe and safeguarded, thereby increasing customer trust and confidence in the dependability of telecommunications services.

Fostering both economic expansion and international connectivity

The synergy between 5G and cloud computing is a driving factor behind economic growth as well as worldwide connection. This goes beyond the consequences that this combination has for technology.

This cooperation provides a suitable climate for entrepreneurship and investment by allowing businesses to operate more efficiently, reach new markets, and deliver innovative products and services. This, in turn, makes the environment more attractive to potential investors. Additionally, the broad use of 5G and cloud technology enables global connectivity, helping to bridge the digital divide and providing people and communities all over the world with access to information and resources that were previously unavailable to them. This interconnection acts as a catalyst for social and economic development. It gives individuals and enterprises the ability to participate in the global economy and contribute to the overall progression of civilization.

The introduction of 5G and cloud computing has ushered in a new era of connectivity, innovation, and transformation in the telecommunications business, which is causing the industry to undergo a revolution. Organizations have the potential to unleash new prospects for growth, development, and progress if they make use of the speed, scalability, and adaptability offered by 5G in conjunction with the power and versatility offered by cloud computing. The synergy between these technologies has far-reaching consequences that extend beyond the field of telecommunications, impacting the future of business, society, and global connection. These implications include empowering IoT and edge computing, as well as improving security and reliability. The world is accelerating its transition into the digital age, and the partnership between fifth-generation wireless (5G) networks and cloud computing is illustrative of the boundless opportunities that can be realized when creativity and technology work together to build a world that is more linked, productive, and prosperous.

2. **Historical Context of Telecommunications**

In the vast tapestry of human history, the development of telecommunications stands as a monument to our inexhaustible hunger for connectivity and communication. This thirst can be seen in the way that telecommunications have evolved over time. The evolution of telecommunications is a fascinating story of human ingenuity, forward movement, and the unyielding will to succeed, beginning with its roots in visual and aural signals and progressing to the present day, when instantaneous worldwide connections are the norm.

The very first methods of human communication

Long before the creation of telephones, computers, or the internet, humans looked for ways to interact with one another despite the distances that separated them physically. This search continues today. An early form of communication was the use of rudimentary signals such as drum beats, smoke signals, and flag semaphore. The discovery of these methods, which enabled humans to send basic messages over great distances, was an essential step in the growth of early groups and civilizations.

Both the Telegraphe and Morse Code were used

Significant leaps forward were made in the ability to communicate over great distances during the 18th and 19th centuries. Both Claude Chappe's creation of the telegraph in 1794, which was a method for transmitting coded messages using electrical impulses, and Samuel Morse's development of Morse code in the 1830s were key milestones in the history of telecommunications. The telegraph was a system for transferring coded messages using electrical impulses. The telegraph and the Morse code made it possible for people to communicate more quickly and reliably across large distances. Messages were transferred down wires by means of a succession of short and long electrical pulses. Due to the fact that this breakthrough made communication across great distances nearly instantaneous, numerous industries, including journalism, finance, and transportation, were completely reshaped as a result.

The revolution brought forth by telephones

Additionally, the telephone, which is widely regarded as one of the greatest game-changing innovations in the annals of telecommunications history, was invented in the 19th century. The invention of the telephone by Alexander Graham Bell in 1876 and subsequent receipt of a patent for it paved the way for a revolution in communication on a worldwide scale. The invention of the telephone radically altered the way in which people communicated with one another since it enabled people to have voice-based discussions in real time despite large distances.

The advent of telephone networks, which were initially composed of manually operated switchboards and were later upgraded to automated exchanges, served as the cornerstone for the development of the contemporary infrastructure for telecommunications. Because of these advancements, the economy was able to expand, and the world became even more interconnected, because individuals and businesses were now able to engage in commerce and keep relationships with people far beyond their own neighborhoods.

Communication Via Radio and Wireless Technologies

The development of wireless communication and radio technology at the beginning of the 20th century brought to other advances in technology. Pioneers such as Guglielmo Marconi were instrumental in the development of wireless telegraphy, which made it possible for communications to be carried via electromagnetic waves across the airwaves. During times of conflict, this technology was extremely useful, since it improved the flow of communication on the battlefield and made it easier to navigate the ocean.

After that, radio broadcasting came into existence, which made it possible for audio material to be transmitted over the airwaves. Radio swiftly emerged as a main medium for the dissemination of news, entertainment, and cultural ideas. In addition to this, it laid the groundwork for future developments in wireless technology, which eventually led to the invention of television and, subsequently, cellular communication.

The Ascent of Television as a Medium

The television, a medium that merged auditory and visual components for the purpose of mass communication, was first introduced around the middle of the 20th century. Televisions quickly became commonplace in homes all over the world, bringing with them the latest news, as well as entertainment and cultural happenings, right into people's living rooms. The broadcasting business experienced exponential growth, and television emerged as a potent medium for the distribution of information, the education of viewers, and the production of entertaining content.

Transmissions Received Via Satellite

The second half of the 20th century witnessed the emergence of satellite communication as a paradigm shifter in the field of global telecommunications. Satellites placed in geostationary orbits made it possible to communicate over great distances, transmit television, and develop global positioning systems. They extended the reach of telecommunications networks beyond the restrictions of terrestrial infrastructure and connected locations that were previously inaccessible or underserved.

The rise of the Internet and the digital revolution.

The advent of the digital age brought about a seismic upheaval in the field of telecommunications around the end of the 20th century and the beginning of the 21st century. The widespread availability of computing devices and the advent of the internet brought about a sea change in how people carried out their daily activities, obtained information, and shared ideas. The development of digital technology made it possible to send enormous volumes of data over great distances, and the advent of the World Wide Web made it possible to connect people and organizations all over the world in unprecedented ways. The creation of e-mail, instant messaging, and, later, various social media platforms occurred concurrently with the expansion of the internet. These advances sped up the pace of communication even further by making it possible to connect in real time, asynchronously, and through many media types.

The Rise of Mobile Technology and the Development of Cellular Communication

The proliferation of mobile communication is widely regarded as one of the most important breakthroughs in the history of telecoms. People now have the ability to interact with one another regardless of where they are or what they are doing thanks to the advent of the cellular network in the middle of the 20th century.

Communication has become more individualized, portable, and easy as a result of the proliferation of mobile phones and, later, smartphones, which revolutionized the way we operate and gained access to information.

The development of 2G, 3G, and 4G networks has resulted in increased data transfer speeds and a broadening of the capabilities of mobile devices. These technological advances paved the way for the widespread adoption of mobile applications, such as social networking, navigation, and e-commerce, all of which have become essential components of contemporary life.

The Beginning of 5G

Presently, we are on the verge of entering the 5G era. The fifth generation of wireless technology is expected to have data transfer rates that have never been seen before, ultra-low latency, and the ability to link a large number of devices all at once. 5G is not merely an improvement over previously available technology; rather, it is a revolution that will determine the course of the future of communications. It has the potential to be the driving force behind cutting-edge technologies such as augmented reality, virtual reality, the internet of things, and smart cities.

The Compatibility of Fifth-Generation Wireless with Cloud Computing

The convergence of fifth-generation wireless (5G) technology and cloud computing has brought the historical context of telecommunications into the current day at this juncture. While the development of telecommunications has been marked by a number of key milestones in linking people and information throughout the course of its history, the confluence of these two technologies holds the possibility of redefining the fundamental nature of what it means to be connected and to communicate.

The near-instantaneous communication made possible by the high-speed and low-latency capabilities of 5G is made possible by the cloud, which also offers the infrastructure necessary to manage and handle the enormous data flows generated by 5G-enabled devices and apps. This synergy results in the formation of a dynamic ecosystem that makes it possible for individuals and organizations to produce and gain access to a wide range of new services, including as telemedicine, smart cities, autonomous vehicles, and immersive entertainment.

3. **Purpose and Scope of the Book**

The raison d'être of a book and the parameters within which it functions are defined by the book's purpose and scope, respectively. There are very few exceptions to this rule, and "5G and Cloud Synergy Transforms Telecommunications" is one of them. This chapter provides a road map for what the reader may anticipate to find within the book's pages by elaborating on the motivations that led to the writing of the book as well as the territories that are the focus of its exploration.

The Reason Behind Writing the Book

The purpose of this book is to educate and inform readers by providing them with a complete understanding of the subtle dynamics and technical aspects of 5G and cloud technologies. Those individuals who are interested in learning the principles as well as the details of these advances might make use of this document as an educational resource.

Illuminate the Synergy: The purpose of this book is to shine light on how 5G and cloud computing might work together to create something that is greater than the sum of their individual parts. It investigates how their interactions magnify each other's effects, so producing a robust ecosystem that has the potential to propel innovation in a variety of fields.

Motivate Innovation: The book motivates entrepreneurs, businesses, and innovators to harness the potential of this synergy for their own projects by offering real-world case studies and examples. Those individuals who are interested in developing ground-breaking applications and services might draw motivation from this resource.

Confronting Obstacles In spite of the fact that it emphasizes the enormous potential of 5G and cloud synergy, the book also digs into the difficulties and factors of concern that are associated with the use of these technologies. It provides readers with the knowledge necessary to negotiate the complicated landscapes of security, privacy, and regulatory challenges.

Envision the Future: As 5G and cloud technologies continue to advance, the purpose of this book is to inspire readers to think about the possibilities and trends that lie ahead for the field of telecommunications. It stimulates conversations about ethical issues, the place of artificial intelligence in society, and the possibilities for technological progress in the following generations of devices.

The Topics Covered in the Book

Aspects of 5G Technology The book starts off by offering an in-depth explanation of 5G technology. This includes discussing its essential characteristics, deployment obstacles, and the variety of use cases and applications that it offers.

The Book Explores the World of Cloud Computing, Explaining Its Services, Models, and Benefits The book explores the world of cloud computing, explaining its services, models, and benefits. The reader will come away with a deeper understanding of the function of the cloud in today's modern telecommunications as well as the profound implications it has for the administration and processing of data.

Convergence of 5G and the Cloud: This chapter focuses on the overarching concept of the book and examines how the technologies of 5G and the cloud may support and enhance one another. It elucidates the significance of the synergy in question as well as the function that computing at the edge plays in the development of a resilient infrastructure.

Transforming Industries: The book demonstrates the revolutionary impact of 5G and cloud synergy across a variety of industries, including healthcare, smart cities, manufacturing, entertainment, and agriculture, by analyzing a variety of case studies. These technologies are altering industries and making people's lives better, and the readers will comprehend how this is happening.

This book guides the reader through the complexity of guaranteeing the security of 5G and cloud networks in a world where the protection of personal data and the prevention of cybercrime are of the utmost importance. It covers ways for protecting data and complying with regulatory requirements in a comprehensive manner.

Connectivity on a Global Scale: The article "5G and Cloud Synergy Transforms Telecommunications" discusses the global repercussions of these technological advancements. It investigates the geopolitical landscape of the telecommunications industry as well as potential methods for bridging the digital divide and enhancing the capabilities of emerging countries.

The Reader is Invited to Contemplate the Future of Telecommunications As the reader progresses through the book, they are given the opportunity to think about the future of telecommunications. Emerging technologies, the impact of artificial intelligence and the Internet of Things, and the ethical considerations that come with living in a hyper-connected world are all topics that are investigated in this book.

The book also dives into the sociological and economic repercussions of telecommunications, examining the implications of these technologies for human growth, ethics, and environmental sustainability. In addition, the book examines the societal and economic impacts of telecommunications.

This book is more than simply a technical guidebook; it is a guide to understanding how the convergence of 5G and cloud computing is transforming the world as we know it. It is titled "5G and Cloud Synergy Transforms Telecommunications" (also known as "5G and Cloud Synergy Transforms Telecommunications"). Whether they are technology enthusiasts, professionals, business executives, policymakers, or just curious minds wanting to comprehend the current change in telecommunications, it aims to inform, inspire, and guide readers.

The reader will go on a journey that traverses the technical intricacies, practical applications, social implications, and emerging possibilities of 5G and cloud synergy in the pages that follow. This journey may be broken down into four categories: practical applications, societal implications, emerging possibilities, and technical subtleties. The goal of this book is to provide readers with the knowledge and insights they require to successfully traverse this fast changing terrain, to fully embrace the promise, and to effectively address the difficulties that lie ahead. This book is designed to be your trusted companion on this thrilling voyage of transformation, whether you are an entrepreneur wanting to exploit emerging technologies for innovation or a concerned citizen considering the influence on society. Regardless of which category you fall into, this book will provide you with the information you need.

4. **Outline of Chapters**

The book "5G and Cloud Synergy Transforms Telecommunications" is structured in the form of a comprehensive sequence of chapters that lead readers through the intricate landscape of 5G and cloud technologies, their convergence, and the transformative influence on telecommunications as well as society in general. The following summary gives an overview of the structure of the book as well as the important ideas that are discussed in each individual chapter:

The development of communications is covered in detail in Chapter 1.

This introductory chapter goes deeper into the historical setting of telecommunications, tracking its development from the earliest forms of communication to the digital era of today. It shines a light on the significant landmarks and technological developments that have helped define the landscape of telecommunications and paves the way for the exploration of 5G and cloud synergy.

Understanding 5G Technology is Covered in Chapter 2

The second chapter provides a comprehensive overview of the 5G technology by elaborating on its core principles, prominent characteristics, and underlying technological foundations. This article investigates the significance of 5G in the context of contemporary telecommunications, focusing on its potential to revolutionize connectivity, data transfer, and the spread of Internet of Things (IoT) devices.

The power of cloud computing is discussed in Chapter 3.

In the context of the field of telecommunications, the purpose of this chapter is to dissect the power that cloud computing possesses. This article sheds light on the several cloud services and deployment methods currently available, illuminating their function in relation to the storage, processing, and administration of data. The reader will obtain an understanding of the advantages of utilizing cloud computing in conjunction with 5G for increased scalability, flexibility, and efficiency.

The Convergence of 5G and the Cloud is Discussed in Chapter 4.

In the fourth chapter, we explore more into the central topic of the converging technologies of 5G and the cloud. It investigates how these two tremendous forces might work together to create a resilient infrastructure that is able to serve a wide variety of innovative applications and services by complementing and reinforcing one another. In addition to this, the chapter looks into the function that edge computing plays in ensuring a smooth connection between 5G networks and the cloud.

"Transforming Industries with 5G and Cloud," is now available in Chapter 5.

This chapter includes a number of case studies and real-world examples that highlight the disruptive impact that the combination of 5G and the cloud can have across a variety of different businesses. The reader will receive insights into how these technologies are transforming operations, expanding efficiency, and improving the overall quality of life in a variety of fields, including healthcare, smart cities, manufacturing, and entertainment.

Security and Privacy in the Era of 5G and the Cloud is the Topic of Chapter 6.

In Chapter 6, we will navigate the complicated terrain of security and privacy in the age of 5G and the cloud. It discusses techniques and best practices for safeguarding sensitive data and ensuring compliance with regulatory frameworks, as well as the problems that are related with securing 5G and cloud networks. The reader will go away with a complete knowledge of the significance of data protection in a world that is becoming increasingly linked.

Global Connectivity and the Fifth Generation Wireless Standard in Chapter 7.

This chapter discusses the worldwide ramifications of technologies such as 5G and the cloud, with a particular emphasis on the roles these technologies play in reducing the digital gap and increasing global connectedness. It digs into the socio-economic impact of new technologies, studying how they can contribute to the empowerment of developing nations and the growth of society on a global scale. Specifically, it focuses on how these technologies can empower women. The geopolitical dynamics of the telecommunications industry are discussed to some extent in this chapter in relation to the rollout of 5G.

The Future of Communications is the Topic of Chapter 8.

In Chapter 8, we encourage readers to think beyond the recent developments in 5G and cloud computing and consider what the future of telecommunications might look like. It investigates new technological developments and trends, such as the impact of artificial intelligence and the Internet of Things, among other topics. Additionally, the chapter goes into the ethical considerations that should be given to future generations of telecommunications technology as well as the potential breakthroughs that may be made in those generations.

The Function of Telecommunications in Modern Society is the Topic of Chapter 9.

The influence of telecommunications on wider aspects of society is the primary topic of discussion in this chapter. It addresses the ethical considerations, cultural ramifications, and environmental sustainability that are connected with the expansion of these technologies, as well as the social and economic repercussions of the synergy between 5G and the cloud. The reader will go away with a comprehensive understanding of the ways in which numerous dimensions of human progress and societal well-being connect with telecommunications.

Concluding Remarks, Chapter 10

The last chapter provides a comprehensive summary of the most important thoughts and takeaways from the rest of the book. It reviews the revolutionary potential of 5G and cloud synergy in the field of telecommunications, putting an emphasis on both the promise and the obstacles that are still to come. The final part of the chapter is a call to action, in which the reader is urged to make use of the knowledge learned from the book in order to successfully traverse the ever-changing environment of the telecommunications industry and to seize the prospects for growth and innovation.

The appendix includes a glossary, a list of acronyms, and references.

An appendix is included in the book, which contains a dictionary of important terms and concepts, a list of pertinent acronyms, as well as a complete list of references and recommended reads for readers who wish to go deeper into certain themes discussed in the book.

In the index:

In addition to this, the book includes an index that acts as a thorough guide to the most important subjects, ideas, and concepts that are explored across the various chapters. The index makes it possible for readers to discover specific material and references in a rapid and efficient manner, which in turn makes it easier for readers to delve further into the book's subject matter.

The article "5G and Cloud Synergy Transforms Telecommunications" provides readers with a roadmap to navigate the convoluted environment of 5G, cloud computing, and the revolutionary impact that both of these technologies will have on the telecoms industry and society as a whole. This roadmap is presented in the form of an organized and complete overview.

Chapter 1

The Evolution of Telecommunications

Throughout the course of human history, there has been a phenomenal development in the science and technology of telecommunications, which is the science and technology of delivering information over large distances. Not only has the evolution of telecommunications transformed the way we communicate, but it has also revolutionized the worlds of business, politics, and society. Some of the earliest forms of communication were smoke signals and semaphore systems, while today's complex 5G networks are the result of this progress. This article delves into the intriguing history of communications, following its historical evolution and technological breakthroughs while also showcasing the significant impact that it has had on our day-to-day lives.

1. **The Earliest Methods of Public Communication**
   Signals in the Smoke and Beats on the Drums
   Our forefathers were able to communicate with one another across great distances in times past by employing simple methods such as smoke signals and drum beats. For instance, indigenous peoples would employ smoke signals to communicate over long distances when they only needed to relay simple information. The proliferation of drums as a means of communication across Africa and other regions made it possible to convey more nuanced ideas through rhythms that were uniquely their own.
   Signaling System Semaphores
   Throughout the course of human history, semaphore systems have been evolved. In these devices, coded messages were transmitted using either flags or mechanical arms. In particular, the Chappe semaphore, which was developed at the end of the 18th century, saw extensive application in France as well as in other areas of Europe.
2. **The Rise of the Telegraph Industry**
   The Morse Code and the Development of the Electric Telegraph

Samuel Morse's development of the electric telegraph in the 19th century marked a significant step forward in human communication. Morse code, which consists of a series of dots and dashes that indicate letters and numbers, makes it possible to communicate more quickly and reliably across large distances. This technology had a significant influence on business and government practices, as well as on military operations.

Seabed Wires and Cables

Midway through the 19th century saw the creation of subsea telegraph lines, which made it possible for people to communicate across oceans. One of the most notable undertakings was the installation of the first cable to across the Atlantic Ocean, connecting Europe and North America. These technological achievements completely revolutionized worldwide communication and the interconnection of the world.

3. **The Age of the Telephone**

The invention of the telephone is credited to Alexander Graham Bell

Alexander Graham Bell received the patent for his groundbreaking invention, the telephone, in the year 1876. The telephone made it possible for people to communicate verbally over large distances. The telephone brought about a rapid and broad shift in the manner in which people interacted with one another as well as conducted business.

Changes that Have Occurred in the Telephone Network

Because of the rapid expansion of the telephone network, the establishment of telephone exchanges and a network of lines that are connected to one another became necessary. The Bell System in the United States, which was famous for its monopoly on telephone service, was an integral part of the process that led to the standardization of the infrastructure for telecommunications.

4. **Communication Via Radio and Wireless Devices**

Marconi and the development of wireless telegraph

Radio communication was invented as a direct result of the work that Guglielmo Marconi did experimenting with wireless telegraphy.

Wireless signal transmission made it possible to communicate without the need for physical cables, which was especially significant in marine and military applications. Wireless transmission of signals made it possible to communicate without the need for physical wires.

First Steps Toward Broadcasting

The introduction of radio transmission in the early 20th century brought about a sea change in the manner in which information and entertainment were disseminated. It resulted in the development of mass media, which played an important role in the process of molding public opinion during times of crisis and conflict.

5. **The Age of Digitalization: The Transition to Digital Telecommunications**
   The Origin and Growth of Digital Signals
   The transformation of analog transmissions into digital ones was a watershed moment in the history of the telecommunications industry. The advent of digital technology made it possible to send data in a more effective manner and prepared the way for the convergence of voice, data, and video transmissions on a single network.
   The birth and development of the internet
   The development of the Internet from ARPANET in the late 1960s led to a sea change in the way people communicate throughout the world. It made instantaneous access to information possible and paved the way for the development of new modes of communication, such as email and instant messaging.
6. **The Revolution in Cellular Technology**
   Initiation into the World of Cellular Networks
   A new era of mobile communications was ushered in with the introduction of cellular networks in the 1980s. People were liberated from their dependence on landlines as a result of the widespread adoption of mobile phones in modern life.
   Recent Developments in Mobile Device Technology
   The earliest cell phones were cumbersome and large, but they quickly gave way to elegant smartphones that could communicate by voice, text, data, and video. Inventions such as touchscreens, mobile applications, and mobile internet access have all been made possible because of the mobile sector.
7. **The Internet of Things (IoT), in particular.**
   Putting the Pieces Together
   The Internet of Things (IoT) refers to the interconnection of commonplace gadgets and objects, which makes it possible for these things to speak with one another and share data. This technology has far-reaching ramifications for a variety of different businesses, including the healthcare industry, the transportation industry, and smart city development.
   Going Beyond 5G
   The deployment of 5G networks holds the promise of wireless connectivity that is both more rapid and more dependable. It is anticipated that it will provide support for a diverse array of applications, including augmented reality, smart grids, and driverless vehicles, among others.
8. **Obstacles and Causes for Concern**
   Confidentiality and safety
   Concerns regarding privacy and security have risen to the forefront as a result of the ever-increasing volume of data being transmitted and the interconnection of various devices. There has never been a time when the demand for comprehensive cybersecurity measures was higher.
   The "Digital Divide"

There are certain people who do not have the same level of access to modern communication technologies. Inequitable global connectivity may be difficult to achieve as a result of the digital divide, which is caused by differences in the availability of infrastructure and the cost of services.

9. **The Prospects for the Field of Communications**

Communication on the Quantum Level

The laws of quantum physics, which form the basis of quantum communication, hold the promise of providing unbreakable encryption and a safe means of information transmission. It has the potential to fundamentally alter how we think about the privacy and safety of our data.

Internet Hosted in Outer Space

Companies such as SpaceX and Amazon are hard at work developing plans to launch constellations of satellites in order to deliver internet service over the globe. It is possible that a space-based internet network might bridge the digital divide by providing internet access to previously unconnected areas.

The Application of Artificial Intelligence to the Field of Telecommunications

The use of artificial intelligence into telecommunications systems holds the possibility of more effective network management, increased customer service, and improved predictive infrastructure maintenance.

Telemedicine and Work at a Distance

The advancement of communications technology will continue to be an essential component of telemedicine, which gives patients access to medical care from a remote location. In a similar vein, the expansion of work that may be done remotely is dependent on the availability of dependable communication networks.

From the rudimentary beginnings of smoke signals and semaphore systems to the high-speed, interconnected world of 5G networks and beyond, the development of telecommunications has been a wonderful journey. Smoke signals and semaphore systems were the forerunners of modern communications. This development has not only altered the manner in which we communicate but has also altered the landscape of the entire world, having an effect on domains as varied as commerce, healthcare, education, and entertainment.

Quantum communication, an internet that is based in space, and artificial intelligence are all technologies that are poised to further transform the telecommunications industry. As we look to the future, the possibilities appear to be limitless. These technological breakthroughs, despite the fact that they carry a great deal of potential, also come with obstacles that are related to issues of privacy, security, and equal access.

The development of modern communication technologies is evidence of the inventiveness of humans and of our never-ending drive to connect with one another, despite the vast distances that exist between us physically. This serves as a timely reminder of the potential that technology possesses to mold our environment and propel forward progress. The path that lies ahead for telecommunications appears to be one that will be both exhilarating and revolutionary, and it is a one that will continue to have an effect on each and every facet of our lives.

1.1 Early Telecommunications Technologies

Telecommunications, the art and science of delivering information over great distances, has a long and illustrious history that can be traced back to the invention of a variety of technologies that made it possible for humans to interact with one another despite the vast distances that separated them. This article examines the development of early methods of communication, beginning with the most basic techniques like smoke signals and progressing all the way up to the revolutionary discovery of the telegraph.

The Communication Methods of Smoke Signals and Drums

Long-distance communication was essential to early human activities such as hunting and defense, and it was required to ensure the species' continued existence. The usage of smoke signals can be traced all the way back to the beginning of communication in its many forms. These signals were utilized by a wide range of ancient cultures, including indigenous peoples of Africa and Asia, in order to communicate over extensive distances. Native American tribes were among those cultures. They were able to convey straightforward information such as warnings or requests for aid by lighting fires and creating distinct patterns of smoke.

Drum communication was an additional primitive method of sending messages over large distances. In Africa, this technique comprised the use of enormous drums with distinctive rhythms that could carry more sophisticated information. It was frequently used to announce events or pass along crucial information to populations that were located in close proximity to one another. These early modes of communication had a restricted capability for relaying specific details, and they were extremely dependent on a clear line of sight as well as suitable weather conditions.

Flags and other visible signals are known as semaphores.

Long-distance communication systems also improved over time alongside the development of society. Semaphore systems, which depended on visual signals employing flags, lights, or mechanical arms, arose as more complex tools for the transmission of information. These systems are still in use today. The delivery of increasingly complicated and comprehensive messages across greater distances was made possible by the use of semaphore systems.

The Chappe semaphore, which was developed by the French engineer Claude Chappe in the latter half of the 18th century, is considered to be one of the most important semaphore systems. This system made use of a number of tall towers that were equipped with pivoting arms. Operators were able to convey messages by putting the arms in a variety of different configurations. These messages were able to be delivered across great distances thanks to a network of semaphore stations that were all connected to one another. During that time period, the Chappe semaphore was quite popular in France and was an integral part of the communication systems utilized by the French military and government.

Transmission through Telegraph and Morse Code

The development of the telegraph in the nineteenth century marked the beginning of a fundamental shift in the nature of long-distance communication. The telegraph was a game-changer in terms of communication technology at the time it was invented since it made it possible to send messages across great distances almost instantly. Samuel Morse and Alfred Vail were two of the most important people in the history of the development of the electric telegraph.

Morse code, a method of encoding letters, numbers, and symbols into a series of dots and dashes, was an essential component in the development of the telegraph and was essential to its success. Because it used a binary form of communication, the telegraph was able to send messages swiftly while maintaining their accuracy. The invention of the telegraph had a significant influence on many facets of society, including the workings of businesses, governments, and military organizations.

The construction of the first transcontinental telegraph line in the United States in 1861 was an important milestone in the development of the telegraph and is considered to be one of the most iconic moments in the history of the telegraph. By connecting the East Coast and the West Coast, this massive undertaking cut the amount of time it took to transfer messages across the continent from several weeks down to just a few minutes. The invention of the telegraph had a significant impact on commercial activity since it made real-time stock market information possible and accelerated the dissemination of news and information.

The Role of Undersea Cables in Worldwide Communication

While the telegraph made it possible to communicate quickly over land, the invention of telegraph wires that ran beneath the ocean completely transformed international communication. The laying of these cables beneath the ocean floor made it possible to communicate across oceans, so linking continents and easing the flow of information around the world.

The successful laying of the first transatlantic cable in 1866, which connected Newfoundland and Ireland, is considered to be one of the most significant achievements in the history of subsea telegraphy. This cable was an important step in the progression of the history of telecommunications since it made it possible for people in North America and Europe to communicate almost instantly with one another.

The installation of subsea telegraph cables allowed for the global connectivity of communication networks, which in turn facilitated the transformation of international diplomacy, commerce, and industry. Additionally, it helped nations and peoples feel more connected to one another on a global scale.

1.2 The Emergence of 3G and 4G

The emergence of 3G (Third Generation) and 4G (Fourth Generation) technology heralded a tremendous leap forward in the field of mobile communication, thereby altering the way in which people communicated with one another, accessed information, and did business while they were on the move. These technological developments not only made quicker data transfer possible, but they also cleared the way for the widespread adoption of mobile internet and a variety of other digital services. This article goes into the history, characteristics, and influence of 3G and 4G technologies, showing the revolutionary implications these technologies have had on society, the economy, and the global telecommunications environment.

The Inception of 3G

Beginning in the early 2000s, the shift from second-generation (2G) to third-generation (3G) mobile networks was initiated in response to efforts made by telecommunications firms to increase the speed of mobile data transmission and meet the growing demand for internet access via mobile devices. Mobile phones have developed into multimedia devices that are able to support a broad variety of data-intensive apps with the debut of 3G technology. These applications go beyond the capabilities of traditional voice and text communication.

Users were able to more easily access the internet, send and receive emails, and participate in video conferences as a direct result of the 3G technology's capacity to give better data transfer speeds. This was one of the most important benefits of the technology. Because of this improvement in data speed and capacity, the groundwork was established for the spread of mobile data services, the streaming of multimedia content, and the early phases of the development of mobile applications.

People's habits regarding the consumption of information and the use of mobile devices underwent a sea change after the advent of 3G technology, which helped to promote a society that is more connected and digital. It reshaped the landscape of industries such as e-commerce, media, and telecoms by fostering the creation of mobile-centric businesses, mobile financial services, and mobile-based entertainment platforms.

Improved Data Transfer Rates Because 3G networks enabled data transfer rates that were several times quicker than their 2G predecessors, users were able to more quickly navigate the internet, download files, and stream multimedia content.

Users are now able to experience video streaming, music downloads, and other forms of high-quality multimedia material on their mobile devices thanks to the multimedia support provided by 3G networks, which eased the incorporation of these functions according to their better data transmission capabilities.

Access to the Internet While on the Move Users are now able to read websites, access online services, and participate in a variety of online activities while they are on the move thanks to the expansion of access to the internet made possible by 3G technology.

Users are now able to connect face-to-face in real time, regardless of their geographical locations, thanks to the advent of video calling and conferencing capabilities, which were made possible by the launch of 3G networks, which opened the way for these capabilities. Video Calling and Conferencing.

The Upgrade to 4G Networks

The transition from third-generation (3G) to fourth-generation (4G) mobile technology was a significant leap in terms of mobile technology, as it brought about data speeds that had never been seen before, increased network stability, and greater user experiences. The fourth-generation cellular network, or 4G technology, was developed in the latter part of the 2000s in response to a growing demand for mobile data services that were both quicker and more efficient. These services include high-definition video streaming, online gaming, and other data-intensive applications.

Long-Term Evolution (LTE), one of the cutting-edge technologies that were used in the construction of 4G networks, enabled customers to experience even faster data transfer rates, reduced network latency, and expanded network capacity. This new invention contributed to the widespread use of mobile broadband and further consolidated the role of mobile devices as important tools for communication, entertainment, and work.

High-Speed Data Transfer 4G networks touted much better data transfer speeds compared to 3G networks, making it possible to stream high-definition films without interruption, download large files in a short amount of time, and play online games with less lag.

Low Latency and Reliability: Real-time interactions were made easier by 4G technology's reduced latency and better network reliability. This made activities like online gaming, video conferencing, and live streaming more fluid and responsive.

Advanced Multimedia Services The spread of advanced multimedia services has been enabled by the increased capabilities of 4G networks. These services include high-quality video streaming, immersive virtual reality experiences, and interactive augmented reality apps.

Mobile Broadband Connectivity: 4G technology was an integral part of the process that led to the proliferation of mobile broadband connectivity. This gave customers the ability to access high-speed internet services on their mobile devices such as smartphones, tablets, and other mobile gadgets.

The shift to 4G technology was the driving force behind the explosive expansion of the mobile app economy. This rise spurred the creation of a diverse range of cutting-edge applications and services that were adapted to take use of the capabilities of high-speed mobile networks. The proliferation of mobile-centric solutions and experiences across a variety of sectors, including the entertainment industry, education, healthcare, and e-commerce, has led to a fundamental shift in both consumer behavior and the dynamics of the market.

Influence on Both Society and Industry

The introduction of third-generation and fourth-generation wireless technologies had a significant effect on society, bringing about major shifts in the ways in which individuals connected with one another, accessed information, and did business. Not only did these developments make continuous communication possible, but they also sparked the development of new digital services, business models, and technological innovations.

Digital Transformation: The widespread adoption of 3G and 4G technologies accelerated the digital transformation of various industries, prompting businesses to embrace mobile-centric strategies, develop mobile applications, and optimize their digital presence to cater to the evolving needs and preferences of consumers. The widespread adoption of 3G and 4G technologies accelerated the digital transformation of various industries.

Mobile Banking and Shopping: The proliferation of mobile banking and shopping has been fueled by the availability of high-speed mobile internet. This has enabled customers to make purchases, carry out financial transactions, and access banking services from the convenience of their mobile devices, thereby empowering them to be more financially independent.

Users increasingly turned to their mobile devices for streaming videos, listening to music, and accessing digital content while on the go. This led to the rise of over-the-top (OTT) media services and streaming platforms. Media Consumption Patterns: The introduction of 3G and 4G technologies revolutionized media consumption patterns.

Productivity and Collaboration: The improved connectivity and communication capabilities offered by 3G and 4G networks facilitated remote collaboration, empowering businesses to adopt flexible work models and enabling employees to work efficiently from remote locations using a variety of collaborative tools and applications. This improved connectivity and communication capability was made possible by the networks.

Individuals have come to rely on their mobile devices for a broad variety of activities, including communication, entertainment, productivity, and online transactions, ever since the seamless integration of 3G and 4G technologies into everyday life sparked the era of mobile-centric lives. These developments not only helped to foster increased connectivity, but they also created the framework for the future development and deployment of even more advanced mobile technologies. In other words, they prepared the ground for the coming of 5G and beyond.

The Future of Communication: 5G and Beyond

As the globe continues to embrace the possibilities given by 3G and 4G technologies, the telecommunications industry is already gearing up for the next phase of mobile development with the introduction of 5G networks. This comes at a time when the world is also continuing to embrace the possibilities offered by 3G and 4G technologies. The advent of 5G technology, which is anticipated to deliver even higher data speeds, extremely low latency, and a greater network capacity, is anticipated to unleash a new wave of innovation, making it possible for transformative applications such as autonomous vehicles, immersive augmented reality experiences, and advanced industrial automation.

The development of 3G and 4G technologies provided the groundwork for the digital transformation of society. These technologies made it possible for a mobile-driven culture to emerge, which has fundamentally altered the ways in which people communicate with one another, do their jobs, and engage with the environment around them. Despite the fact that the world is eagerly awaiting the broad deployment of 5G technology and the prospects that it will offer, the legacy of 3G and 4G remains interwoven in the fabric of modern telecommunications, serving as a tribute to the unrelenting pursuit of connectivity, innovation, and technological development.

1.3 The Need for 5G and Cloud Synergy

The convergence of 5G wireless technology with cloud computing is an innovative synergy that has the potential to completely transform the ways in which we connect with one another, interact with one another, and conduct business in today's increasingly digital world. In the following paragraphs, we will discuss the necessity of this merger, the opportunities it creates, and the revolutionary effect it will have on industry, society, and the economy on a worldwide scale.

Acquiring Knowledge about the 5G Technology

The most recent version of wireless communication technology is known as 5G, which is an abbreviation for the phrase "Fifth Generation." In comparison to its predecessors (2G, 3G, and 4G), it claims to be able to transfer data at quicker speeds, to have lower latency, and to have a larger network capacity. With 5G, we are not simply watching an incremental increase in mobile communication; rather, it marks a quantum leap in connection that has far-reaching ramifications. In other words, we are not simply witnessing an incremental improvement in mobile communication.

Data Transfer Rates That Are Extremely High: 5G networks are capable of transferring data at rates of up to 20 gigabits per second (Gbps), which is nearly 100 times quicker than 4G networks. Because of this speed, it is possible to play online games in real time, stream high-definition video without any interruptions, and download files almost instantly.

Low Latency: 5G networks promise dramatically decreased latency, with response times as low as 1 millisecond in some cases. Applications such as autonomous vehicles, telemedicine, and virtual reality all require communication that is nearly instantaneous in order to function properly.

Massive Network Capacity: Because 5G networks are able to handle a significantly larger number of connected devices at the same time, they are ideally suited for applications related to the Internet of Things (IoT). This enables the connectivity of a vast number of devices, ranging from intelligent home appliances to sensors used in industrial settings.

Reliability: Because 5G technology provides greater network reliability, it is appropriate for mission-critical applications in a variety of industries, including healthcare, public safety, and manufacturing.

The Function of Computing in the Cloud

Cloud computing is an established technology that involves the distribution of computer services such as servers, storage, databases, networking, and software over the internet. These services can be accessed from anywhere in the world. Because of this technology, businesses are now able to store data, retrieve that data, and execute programs on remote servers, completely removing the requirement for physical infrastructure.

Scalability is the capability of cloud services to be readily scaled up or down to suit shifting demands. This enables businesses to fulfill such expectations in a flexible and cost-effective manner.

Cloud computing minimizes the need for businesses to invest in and maintain their physical infrastructure, which enables firms to pay only for the computer resources that they actually use. This results in improved cost efficiency.

Access from Anywhere: Since cloud services can be accessed from any location with an internet connection, they make it possible to operate remotely and increase the availability of data and applications.

Data safety and dependability are two of the most important concerns for the leading cloud service providers, thus they put a significant amount of money into redundant infrastructure and various security precautions.

The Synergy: Fifth-Generation Wireless and Cloud Computing

Data Intensity: As the consumption and output of data continues to expand at an exponential rate, there is a demand for networks that are both quicker and more dependable in order to support applications that require a great deal of data. 5G gives the speed and dependability that is required, while cloud computing provides the storage and processing capabilities that are necessary for managing large amounts of data.

Applications such as augmented reality, virtual reality, driverless vehicles, and remote surgery all require very low latency in order to perform properly. The low latency of 5G, when combined with the processing power of cloud computing, guarantees that these applications may be run without any interruptions or vulnerabilities.

Connectivity in the Internet of Things The explosion in the number of Internet of Things devices calls for the development of networks that are able to handle a very large number of connections. The capacity of 5G to manage a large number of devices, in conjunction with cloud-based platforms, makes it possible to manage and analyze data from the Internet of Things in an effective manner.

Edge computing is a paradigm that processes data closer to the source, and it is becoming increasingly important for applications that need to make decisions in real time. Edge computing is another area that benefits from the synergy between 5G and cloud computing. 5G enables rapid data transfer to and from the cloud, which can then be used for processing and analysis.

The Effects on Different Sectors of the Economy and Society

The low latency of 5G will make telemedicine and remote surgery more practicable in the medical field. This will allow surgeons and other medical professionals to conduct procedures or consultations remotely. Cloud-based medical records will make patient information safe to access while also ensuring its confidentiality.

Vehicles Capable of Operating Themselves: The transmission and processing of data must be completed in real time for autonomous vehicles. The combination of 5G connectivity and cloud computing will make it possible for these cars to communicate with one another and with central systems, so ensuring that transportation will be both safe and efficient.

Manufacturing: The manufacturing sector may take advantage of 5G for Internet of Things connectivity and remote monitoring of machinery, while cloud computing handles data analytics and process optimization.

In the realm of entertainment, high-quality streaming services, applications for augmented and virtual reality, and cloud gaming will become even more immersive and accessible to users.

Education: With 5G and cloud resources, educators will be able to conduct virtual classes with little latency, and students will have access to high-quality educational materials from anywhere in the world.

The combination of 5G wireless technology and cloud computing will make it possible to manage cities more effectively, including the control of traffic, the management of trash, and the monitoring of environmental conditions.

Agriculture: Precision agriculture, which is dependent on Internet of Things sensors and real-time data, will become more effective with 5G and cloud-based analytics thanks to advancements in both of these areas.

Business Operations: Companies may reap the benefits of 5G and cloud computing for remote work, collaborative apps, data analysis, and process automation through the use of these technologies.

The ability to access real-time information, such as video streams and data analysis, will be provided to first responders in the public safety sector in order to facilitate more efficient responses to emergency situations.

Concerns and Things to Take Into Account

Security: As our reliance on these technologies continues to grow, maintaining security and protecting the privacy of our data becomes increasingly important. The protection of data and the maintenance of users' privacy both call for stringent security precautions.

Infrastructure: The deployment of 5G infrastructure calls for significant investments, and it is possible that rural areas would experience difficulties in achieving the same degree of connectivity as urban areas.

Cloud computing may involve the storing of data in servers that are situated in multiple areas or even countries. This raises the question of data sovereignty. Concerns over the sovereignty of data and adherence to legislation are raised as a result of this.

Energy Consumption: The infrastructure required for 5G and cloud computing may require a significant amount of energy. In order to lessen our impact on the environment, we need to come up with solutions that are energy-efficient.

The requirements of our ever-more-digital environment are the primary impetus behind the requirement for a synergy between 5G and cloud computing. This combination enables the subsequent wave of technological progress since it provides quicker data rates, lower latency, and a vastly increased capacity for the network. It will revolutionize entire industries, raise people's standards of living, and propel economic expansion. As we move forward, it is vital to address concerns connected to security, infrastructure, data sovereignty, and energy consumption in order to ensure the responsible and sustainable deployment of these technologies. These challenges must be addressed in order for the deployment of these technologies to be sustainable. The convergence of fifth-generation wireless (5G) networks and cloud computing will provide a revolutionary force that will drive future connectivity and creativity.

1.4 The Role of Connectivity in Modern Society

Connectivity is an important factor in the formation of modern civilization because we live in an information age. The impact of connectedness is seen in almost every aspect of our lives, including how we obtain information, how we work, how we interact with the world, and how we communicate.

This article investigates the many functions that connectedness plays in today's society, focusing on the ways in which it affects communication, education, business, healthcare, and interpersonal relationships.

1. **Communication: A Bridge Across Both Physical Distances and Cultural Barriers**

   Connectivity has fundamentally altered the ways in which people communicate, removing boundaries based on geography and making instantaneous global communication possible. The proliferation of the internet, social media, and mobile devices has made it feasible for people to maintain real-time connections with friends and family members who live on different continents. The use of social networks, voice calls, video conferencing, instant messaging, and other forms of real-time communication are now ingrained in our everyday routines.

   In addition, connectivity has helped to develop cross-cultural contacts, making it possible for people to communicate with others who come from a variety of backgrounds and educating them on a variety of points of view. Our perspectives have been broadened, and the amount of cultural interaction has increased, which has contributed to an improvement in our awareness of global issues.

2. **Education: Access to Information and Online-Based Learning**
   The rise of connectivity has brought about a revolution in education by rendering previously inaccessible knowledge more readily available and modifiable. The internet is home to a plethora of educational materials, including digital libraries, research databases, and research databases, as well as online courses and video lessons. Students and others who are learning throughout their lives have access to a wide variety of resources that can help them improve their education and their professional development.
   E-learning platforms like Massive Open Online Courses (MOOCs), which provide individuals all over the world with access to education of a high standard, have proliferated as a direct result of increased connectivity. Education is made more accessible to more people by removing the requirement that students attend classes in person in order to earn degrees and certifications from prominent colleges.
3. **Improving Productivity While Expanding Our Scope in the Business World**
   Connectivity has developed into an essential component of running a business in this day and age. It enables businesses to enhance their productivity by streamlining their procedures, making it easier for employees to work remotely, and so on. Employees are able to operate from any location because to the availability of communication tools, cloud computing, and digital collaboration platforms. They also have access to the data and applications they need.
   E-commerce has flourished as a result of increased connectivity, which enables enterprises to access customers all over the world. The process by which businesses market and sell their goods and services has been revolutionized by the rise of online marketplaces, digital payment methods, and customized advertising. Connectivity is also the driving force behind data analytics, which provides significant insights into the behavior of consumers and trends in the market.
4. **Health care, including telemedicine and remote monitoring of patients**
   Connectivity is paving the way for a revolution in healthcare by opening the door to telemedicine and other forms of remote patient care. Patients now have the ability to receive medical advice, speak with healthcare specialists via video chats, and monitor chronic diseases without having to leave the comfort of their own homes. The collecting and evaluation of real-time health data is made possible by technologies such as mobile apps, wearable technology, and remote patient monitoring devices.
   In addition, connectivity has made it easier for healthcare personnel to share medical information with one another, which has improved teamwork and the quality of care provided to patients. Health information exchanges (HIEs) and electronic health records (EHRs) both make patient data more accessible while simultaneously increasing its level of security. This, in turn, leads to improved decision-making and care coordination.

5. **Social Interactions, Including Participation in Online Communities and Social Media**
   Through the use of social media and other online communities, connectivity has fundamentally altered the ways in which we engage in conversation with one another. People are able to interact with one another, share their experiences, and engage in conversation with a wide variety of people through the use of social platforms. Connectivity has made the globe a smaller and more connected place, allowing for things like renewing old connections, joining communities based on shared interests, and taking part in conversations taking place all over the world.
   These platforms have also evolved into effective instruments for lobbying, raising awareness, and effecting social change. Individuals are able to come together in the pursuit of common objectives and effect positive change because to the increased internet connectedness that enables it. Movements, both local and global, acquire momentum as a result.
6. **Aspects of Amusement: Content Available for Streaming and On-Demand**
   Because of increased connectivity, the entertainment business has been completely revolutionized by the availability of content that can be accessed on demand. Streaming services for media such as music, movies, and TV shows, as well as video games, have emerged as the industry standard. It is no longer necessary for consumers to consume their preferred content on physical media or at predetermined times because they may do so whenever and whenever they desire.
   Connectivity has also led to the development of platforms for user-generated content, which enable users to generate, distribute, and earn money from their own content. Connectivity has given content makers more power and has helped democratize the entertainment sector, which can be seen everywhere from YouTube to podcasts.
7. **Transportation: Satellite Navigation and Advanced Vehicle Technology**

Connectivity has opened the door to innovative approaches to mobile mobility in the field of transportation. Traveling has become less time consuming and more convenient as a result of innovations like as GPS navigation, ridesharing apps, and real-time traffic information. Connectivity also plays an important part in the development of driverless vehicles, which will make transportation both safer and more accessible.

Connectivity is utilized in smart cities in order to improve urban planning, maximize the flow of traffic, and significantly cut down on energy consumption. The use of sensors, data analysis, and connected infrastructure all contribute to creating urban landscapes that are more sustainable and habitable.

Concerns and Things to Take Into Account

While modern civilization can reap many benefits from increased connection, there are also a number of obstacles and factors to take into consideration.

The term "digital divide" refers to the fact that not everyone has the same access to various forms of online connectivity. Access to the internet and other digital technologies can be unequally distributed, which can worsen inequalities in education, employment, and healthcare that already exist.

Concerns concerning a person's right to their data's privacy and their online safety are brought up by an increase in connectivity. The gathering and transmission of personally identifiable information can result in breaches of privacy and vulnerabilities, which is why strict safeguards and laws are required.

Overload of Information Both the constant flow of information and the relationships that take place on social networking sites can contribute to information overload, which in turn can lead to mental health problems. The positive aspects of increased connection must not be prioritized at the expense of the potential drawbacks.

Dependency: Relying excessively on a digital connection might put one at risk of developing dependency and addiction, which can have negative effects on one's relationships, level of productivity, and general well-being. It is crucial to set digital limits and manage the amount of time spent looking at screens.

Chapter 2

Understanding 5G Technology

In this period of rapid technological growth, the 5G technology stands out as one of the most revolutionary innovations. It holds the potential to alter the way in which we connect, communicate, and interact with the digital world. This all-encompassing book attempts to present an in-depth overview of 5G technology by investigating its fundamentals, technological underpinnings, applications, and its far-reaching ramifications across a variety of businesses and facets of our day-to-day life.

Before we begin:

The Concept of the 5G Technology

The word "5G" refers to the fifth generation of wireless technology, which follows in the footsteps of the 4G (LTE) generation. It is the standard that represents the most recent and cutting-edge version of mobile communication technology. In comparison to its predecessors, 5G technology is expected to provide faster data transfer speeds, lower latency, more network capacity, and increased dependability. It is anticipated that these improvements will have a significant impact on a variety of business sectors as well as areas of day-to-day life.

The Development of Cordless and Wireless Communication

It is vital to trace the growth of wireless communication in order to have an understanding of the relevance of the 5G technology. From the analog cellular networks of the first generation (1G) all the way up to the long-term evolution (LTE) networks of the fourth generation (4G), each generation has brought about considerable advancements in both the speed of data transmission and the capabilities of the network. We are currently experiencing a quantum leap in wireless technology with the introduction of 5G, which will make it possible to deliver innovative apps and services.

Components Crucial to the Operation of the 5G Network

The Spectrum of Millimeter Waves

The utilization of millimeter-wave (mmWave) spectrum is recognized as one of the most important aspects of 5G technology.

These bands operating at higher frequencies provide a wider bandwidth as well as faster data transfer speeds. On the other hand, mmWave signals have a short range and are easily disrupted by physical obstructions such as walls and trees. Conquering these obstacles is absolutely necessary to ensure the success of 5G networks.

Massive MIMO is an extension of the multiple-input, multiple-output technique.

Massive MIMO is a technology that employs the utilization of numerous antennas on both the transmitting and receiving ends of a communication link. This allows for increased data throughput and lower latency. Wireless networks see a huge increase in both their efficiency and their capacity as a result of this method. It makes possible the practice of spatial multiplexing, which refers to the transmission of many data streams simultaneously and results in connections that are both quicker and more reliable.

Formation of beams

Beamforming is a method of signal processing that is utilized in 5G technology. The purpose of this method is to concentrate radio waves in a particular direction, so producing a "beam" of signal. This technology allows for more exact targeting of devices, which in turn helps to reduce interference and improves the efficiency of the network.

Slicing of the Network

The term "network slicing" refers to a feature of 5G that makes it possible to partition a single physical network into several different virtual networks. Each virtual network can be tailored to fulfill a particular need, such as providing enhanced mobile broadband (eMBB) for high-speed data transfer or ultra-reliable low-latency communication (URLLC) for mission-critical applications.

Computing on the Edge

Computing at the network's edge is an essential element of 5G technology. It involves processing data in a location that is geographically closer to its origin, which helps to reduce latency and enables real-time applications. This is particularly important for services such as automated factories and self-driving cars.

Miniature Cells

Traditional cell towers are complemented with smaller, more compact base stations known as small cells. They are installed in places with a high population density in order to boost the capacity of the network and the coverage it provides. Small cells are absolutely necessary to ensure that 5G networks can provide constant high-speed connectivity in metropolitan areas, and they play a pivotal part in this process.

Recent Developments in 5G Technology

Enhancements to Both Speed and Latency

When compared to 4G technology, the data transfer speeds offered by 5G technology are substantially faster. 5G networks have the potential to give download speeds in the gigabit range, with some estimates estimating that they might even reach up to 20 Gbps. 4G networks normally provide download speeds of up to 100 Mbps. Real-time communication can be achieved using systems that have a lower latency, on the order of one millisecond or less; examples of such systems are autonomous vehicles and virtual reality.

Increased Productivity Across Networks

In order to lessen the impact of wireless communication on the environment, energy-saving features built into 5G networks will be utilized. This is made possible by the utilization of technologies such as dynamic spectrum sharing, which enables a variety of wireless devices to coexist on the same frequency range.

Spectrum Assignments and Their Functions

5G networks make use of a much wider spectrum of frequencies, which includes the mmWave bands, sub-6 GHz bands, and unlicensed spectrum that was previously discussed. Because of the diversity of the spectrum, 5G networks will be able to provide both high-speed, short-range connectivity in urban areas (mmWave) and larger coverage with good speed (sub-6 GHz).

Examples of Uses for the 5G Technology

Increased Capacity for Mobile Broadband (eMBB)

One of the most important applications for 5G technology is enhanced mobile broadband (eMBB). Users will be able to watch high-definition videos while streaming, download large files, and effortlessly use applications that require a lot of data if this mission is successful in delivering much quicker and more dependable mobile broadband connectivity. This is especially important for customers and companies who rely on mobile data to conduct their daily operations.

Communication with an Ultra-Low Delay and High Reliability (URLLC)

URLLC was developed specifically for use in applications that require an exceptionally low amount of latency along with high levels of reliability. This include things like telemedicine, automated cars, factory automation, and mission-critical communication in fields like public safety.

The low latency and high reliability offered by 5G make it feasible for devices and systems to connect with one another with a minimal amount of lag, thereby improving both safety and productivity.

mMTC, which stands for massive machine type communication

In the context of the Internet of Things (IoT), the connectivity of a very large number of devices is referred to as mMTC. The Internet of Things (IoT) can handle a large scale of linked devices thanks to the capabilities of 5G technology, which includes everything from smart sensors and wearables to connected appliances. mMTC is distinguished by its unique capacity to connect a great number of devices all at once while preserving the life of the battery.

IoT stands for the Internet of Things.

The Internet of Things (IoT) is an ecosystem of connected gadgets and sensors that is expanding at a rapid rate. IoT applications are made possible by 5G technology because it provides the necessary connectivity, low latency, and capacity to connect and manage an ever-expanding array of devices. This is a vital role in the process of enabling IoT applications. This extends to applications for the Internet of Things in the industrial sector, as well as smart cities and residences.

The 5G Revolution and Its Impact on Industry

Concerning medical care

Telemedicine, remote patient monitoring, and augmented reality-assisted procedures are just a few examples of how the healthcare industry stands to benefit from the rollout of 5G technology. It is possible to send vital health data in real time because to the low latency and high dependability of 5G networks. This results in healthcare services that are both more effective and more easily accessible.

Industrial Production

The concept of Industry 4.0, which is defined by smart factories, automation, and real-time data processing, is made possible in the manufacturing industry by the introduction of 5G. Industrial robotics and machinery will be able to be operated with greater accuracy as a result of the ultra-reliable and low-latency communication capabilities offered by 5G. This will result in increased production efficiency and decreased downtime.

Transportation and Advanced Urban Planning

The development of autonomous vehicles and intelligent transportation systems relies heavily

on the technology of fifth-generation wireless (5G). Real-time communication between cars, infrastructure, and control centers requires both low latency and high-speed connectivity, all of which are supplied by 5G networks. 5G is being utilized in smart cities to improve the effectiveness of traffic control, energy saving, and public safety programs.

To educate

5G makes it possible for students to learn remotely by giving them access to high-quality educational materials and the ability to communicate in real time with their teachers. This technology extends beyond the confines of conventional schools, making it easier for people to receive an education even if they live in isolated or underdeveloped places.

The Entertainment Industry and the Media

The introduction of high-speed, low-latency connectivity for immersive experiences like augmented and virtual reality is one of the ways that 5G will change the entertainment and media industries. This paves the way for the development of new gaming, streaming, and content consumption experiences that are interactive.

The agricultural industry

Precision farming is made possible in the agricultural sector by the use of Internet of Things (IoT) sensors and real-time data analysis. Through the use of 5G connection, farmers are able to better monitor crop conditions, automate irrigation systems, and increase productivity.

Concerns and Things to Take Into Account

Deployment of Infrastructure In order to roll out 5G infrastructure, major investments need to be made, and a significant amount of small cells and base stations need to be deployed. It's possible that not all regions and rural areas would receive the same level of connectivity as metropolitan areas. This could be an issue for some locations.

Concerns concerning data security and privacy have been raised in response to the growing reliance on 5G technology. In order to prevent data breaches and vulnerabilities, it is imperative that the gathering and transport of sensitive data be encrypted.

Spectrum Allocation The process of allocating spectrum for 5G networks is a complex one that needs coordination among network operators, governments, and regulators. The full promise of 5G cannot be realized without effective utilization of the spectrum.

Energy Consumption: The infrastructure that is required for 5G networks is capable of using a significant amount of energy. It is essential to find solutions that are energy-efficient if we are to reduce our negative effects on the environment.

The fact that not everyone has the same level of access to 5G technology has contributed to the existence of a digital gap. It is necessary to make an effort to close this gap and guarantee that everyone has equal access to high-speed connectivity.

The advent of 5G technology represents a significant turning point in the development of wireless communication. This new technology offers increased data transfer rates, less lag time, and a wide range of potential applications in a variety of fields. Its influence may be felt in a variety of fields, including medicine, industry, transportation, education, entertainment, and agriculture, and it is reshaping the way we work and live. It is vital to solve difficulties related to infrastructure, security, privacy, spectrum allocation, and energy usage in order to ensure responsible and sustainable deployment of 5G technology as the globe continues to adopt it. The convergence of 5G networking technology and newly developing applications holds the potential to open up hitherto unexplored doors and transform entire industries, thereby boosting the ways in which we connect to one another, communicate with one another, and engage with the digital world.

2.1 What is 5G?

Communication networks are the vital organs of our increasingly interconnected world in this age of digital technology. The development of wireless technology has been an essential factor in the way that we connect with one another, exchange information, and interact with one another. The introduction of 5G, the fifth generation of wireless technology, is one of the most important developments that has taken place in the most recent few years. The advent of 5G has the potential to completely alter our day-to-day lives, since it will bring with it significantly increased download speeds, decreased lag times, and a plethora of cutting-edge software options. In this post, we will discuss what 5G is, its important features, and the possible impact that it could have on a variety of businesses as well as on life in general.

The Meaning of 5G

The acronym 5G refers to the upcoming fifth generation of wireless technology, which will replace 4G (LTE) networks. When compared to its forerunners, 5G is not only an incremental update; rather, it represents a significant step forward in terms of performance, capabilities, and breadth. In comparison to 4G, which increased internet speeds and made it possible for more people to use mobile applications, 5G raises the bar for wireless communication to an entirely new level. It provides a comprehensive set of enhancements, which positions it as the foundation upon which future technical advances will be built.

Characteristics of 5G Networks

Increased Data speeds One of the most distinguishing characteristics of 5G is that it offers dramatically increased data speeds. While 4G networks provide download rates in the tens of megabits per second (Mbps), 5G networks have the potential to produce download speeds in the gigabit range and beyond. This is made possible by employing cutting-edge technology such as Massive Multiple Input Multiple Output (MIMO) and millimeter-wave (mmWave) frequencies in the transmission of data.

5G has been shown to significantly cut down on the latency experienced by networks. The term "latency" refers to the amount of time it takes for data to move from its origination point to its final location. The goal of 5G networks is to reach a latency of as little as one millisecond, which will make it easier to implement real-time applications such as remote surgery, augmented reality, and virtual reality.

Enhanced Connectivity: 5G networks offer enhanced connectivity in places with a high population density. Because it is capable of simultaneously managing a greater number of devices, it is ideally suited for use in smart cities, applications for the Internet of Things (IoT), and enormous machine-to-machine communication.

Dependability: 5G networks are intended to have a higher level of dependability compared to their predecessors. This is absolutely necessary for mission-critical applications like remote industrial control systems and autonomous car control systems.

Energy Efficiency 5G is more energy efficient than previous generations of wireless networking technology, which helps to lessen the negative effects that wireless networks have on the environment while also extending the battery life of mobile devices.

The Implications and Applications

Improved Mobile Experiences 5G networks improve mobile experiences by making it possible to

download and upload data at higher rates, stream video more smoothly, and reduce the amount of time it takes for apps to respond. Better mobile gaming, video conferencing, and media consumption are the results of this development.

The Internet of Things will undergo a revolutionary change as a result of the exponential development that 5G will enable. The capacity of 5G to connect enormous numbers of devices in a seamless manner will transform the way in which we interact with the world around us. This will affect everything from smart homes and cities to industrial automation and healthcare.

Vehicles Capable of Operating Without Human Intervention 5G is a Critical Enabler for Doing So. The low latency and high dependability of 5G networks make it possible for vehicles to connect with one another and with the infrastructure supporting traffic in real time. This makes transportation more secure and more effective.

Healthcare: 5G will make telemedicine and remote surgery more accessible by allowing medical personnel to do sophisticated treatments from a distance while experiencing minimum latency. Telemedicine and remote surgery are two examples. The technology also makes it possible to monitor patients in real time, which contributes to an improvement in the delivery of healthcare.

The fifth-generation wireless (5G) network is an essential component in the development of smart cities. The connectivity provided by 5G networks has the potential to revolutionize city life in a number of ways, including environmental monitoring, intelligent traffic management, public safety, and energy efficiency.

In the field of education, 5G will make it possible to have learning experiences that are more immersive and engaging. The use of augmented reality and virtual classrooms, as well as remote access to educational resources, are all becoming more productive and interesting.

Obstacles and Causes for Concern

Investing in Infrastructure: The implementation of 5G involves significant infrastructure changes, including the installation of tiny cells, which can be time-consuming and expensive.

Spectrum Allocation: A global challenge that must be met is the allocation of sufficient spectrum for 5G networks. It is necessary for governments and regulatory agencies to find a middle ground in order to satisfy the requirements of a variety of industries while still maintaining a consistent global standard.

Security: The enhanced connectivity that 5G will bring about may result in the introduction of new security risks. The protection of data against cyber threats and the maintenance of data privacy are of the utmost importance.

The digital gap is likely to be exacerbated by the rollout of fifth-generation wireless networks (5G), as these networks may not be available to all populations, particularly in underserved and rural regions.

The fifth-generation wireless (5G) standard is not merely an innovation in technology; rather, it is a driver of revolutionary shifts in the ways in which we work and live. 5G is poised to reinvent industries, facilitate innovation, and improve the quality of life for billions of people all over the world as a result of its high-speed, low-latency connectivity and potential to support a wide range of applications. The promise that 5G technology holds cannot be denied, as it provides a look into a future that is quicker, more connected, and more intelligent than ever before. Despite the hurdles it faces, the promise of 5G technology cannot be denied. It is crucial that stakeholders work together to address difficulties and ensure fair access in order to allow everyone to realize the benefits of this exciting technological revolution as 5G continues to roll out and mature.

2.2 Key Features and Benefits of 5G

The world is on the verge of experiencing a connection revolution, and at the vanguard of this transition is 5G, also known as the fifth generation of wireless technology. It is expected that 5G will radically alter the ways in which we connect to one another, communicate with one another, and engage with the digital world as it continues to be rolled out over the world. In this essay, we will discuss the most important characteristics and advantages of 5G, which are poised to transform many different fields of business and life in general.

Characteristics of 5G Networks

At Breakneck Speeds:

The incredible speed that 5G possesses is one of its most notable characteristics. In contrast to 4G networks, which typically provide download speeds in the tens of megabits per second (Mbps), 5G networks have the potential to give download speeds in the gigabit range and beyond. This huge improvement in data transfer speeds is made possible by utilizing cutting-edge technology such as Massive Multiple Input Multiple Output (MIMO) and millimeter-wave frequencies (mmWave). Because of this lightning-fast connectivity, tasks like downloading large files, streaming high-definition entertainment, and utilizing programs that require a lot of data may be completed in what feels like no time at all.

Extremely Low Latencies:

The goal of 5G is to reduce network latency to an extent that has never been seen before. The term "latency" refers to the amount of time it takes for data to move from its origination point to its final location. The latency of 5G networks can be as low as one millisecond, which is a significant improvement above the latency of 4G networks. Real-time applications, such as remote surgery, augmented reality, and virtual reality, require low latency in order to function properly. It ensures that actions begun in the digital sphere have a nearly instantaneous impact in the actual world, which enables the creation of new applications and experiences.

Enhanced Connectivity in Highly Populated Areas:

One of the most important aspects of 5G is its capacity to improve connectivity in locations with a high population density. Congestion is a common issue for traditional networks in densely populated urban locations as well as for large events. Because of its greater capacity and the ability to slice the network, 5G is capable of handling a significantly bigger number of connected devices at the same time. This is essential for the development of smart cities, applications for the Internet of Things (IoT), and the ever-increasing number of gadgets that people use in their everyday lives, such as smartphones and smart appliances.

Both in terms of availability and dependability:

The next-generation 5G wireless networks are planned to provide a higher degree of dependability than their predecessors. This reliability is absolutely necessary for mission-critical applications like driverless vehicles and remote control systems for industrial facilities. Industries that demand continuous and stable connectivity stand to benefit significantly from the increased reliability that 5G provides. Additionally, the technology offers improved network availability, which in turn reduces both downtime and disruptions to service.

Efficiency in the Use of Energy:

Energy efficiency, resolving environmental problems, and extending the battery life of mobile devices are all high priorities for 5G, which lays a major emphasis on these areas. The energy-efficient design of 5G is an important step in the right direction at a time when people all across the world are becoming more aware of the influence that technology has on the environment. This function is beneficial to users as well as the environment because it allows devices to go longer between charges and reduces the amount of energy that is consumed.

The advantages of 5G

Improved Performance on Mobile Devices:

The transition to 5G will result in a much enhanced mobile experience. Mobile gaming, video conferencing, and media consumption are all made more pleasurable and convenient by faster download and upload speeds, smoother video streaming, and quicker app reaction times. 5G is the foundation for mobile innovation since it makes possible the development of new applications and services that were previously impossible to implement owing to the constraints of existing networks.

The Revolution of IoT:

With the introduction of 5G, the Internet of Things is about to experience explosive growth. The capability of 5G to link a large number of devices in a seamless manner is essential to the transformation of how we interact with our surroundings. This includes smart homes and cities, as well as industrial automation and medical care. It will enable a network of intelligent devices that can collect and share data in real time, which will revolutionize a number of different industries.

Vehicles That Drive Themselves:

The development of fully autonomous vehicles is greatly aided by the implementation of 5G. The low latency and high dependability of 5G networks make it possible for vehicles to connect with one another and with the infrastructure supporting traffic in real time. This makes transportation more secure and more effective. This technique paves the way for self-driving automobiles that are not only safer but also more technologically advanced.

The Transformation of Healthcare:

Telemedicine and remote surgery become more accessible in the medical field with the introduction of 5G. This is because medical experts are able to carry out intricate procedures from a distance with little latency. The technology also makes it possible to monitor patients in real time, which improves both the quality of medical care and the outcomes for patients.

Cities that are Smart:

The impact that 5G will have on smart cities will be significant. It is beneficial for intelligent traffic management, monitoring of the environment, maintaining public safety, and increasing energy efficiency. Cities have the potential to become more environmentally friendly, connected, and responsive to the requirements of their citizens if they adopt 5G technology.

Instructional Technology and Distant Studying:

The advent of 5G is set to bring about a sea change in the educational system by making it possible to engage in more immersive and interactive forms of instruction. Education is made more available and useful as a result of technological advancements such as virtual classrooms, augmented reality, and remote access to educational resources.

The introduction of 5G will fundamentally alter the landscape of wireless communication. As a result of its lightning-fast download times, incredibly low latency, vastly increased connectivity, and rock-solid dependability, 5G is poised to completely transform a variety of sectors and aspects of day-to-day life. The benefits of 5G are extensive, ranging from improving the mobile experience to allowing the Internet of Things, driverless vehicles, and breakthroughs in healthcare.

It is critical that governments, corporations, and individuals work together to provide equal access and address the issues associated with this disruptive technology in order to pave the way for a more connected and innovative future. As it continues to roll out and mature, it is important to note that this technology is expected to have a significant impact on many facets of society.

2.3 5G Deployment Challenges

The launch of 5G technology has been widely anticipated, as it promises to usher in previously unimaginable breakthroughs in connectivity as well as revolutionary shifts across all sectors of the economy. The rollout of 5G networks, on the other hand, is not without its share of difficulties. In this article, we will discuss the complex landscape of 5G deployment issues, which range from technical impediments to regulatory concerns. We will also discuss how important it is to overcome these obstacles in order to unlock the full potential of 5G.

Problems of a Technical Nature

Reconstruction of the Infrastructure:

The requirement for a significant infrastructure makeover is one of the most significant technological issues associated with the introduction of 5G. To fulfill its promises of high speeds and low latency, 5G will, in contrast to earlier generations of wireless technology, call for a more densely packed network of base stations and tiny cells. The installation of such a comprehensive infrastructure, which is often carried out in highly populated regions, is an operation that is both expensive and time-consuming.

The Spectrum of Millimeter Waves:

Millimeter wave (mmWave) frequencies, which allow for high-speed connections, face a number of issues when they are used. These frequencies have far limited ranges of propagation, and their signals are easily disrupted by things like walls and trees. As a result, the deployment of mmWave networks necessitates meticulous planning as well as an increased number of base stations.

Capacity of the Backhaul Network:

Backhaul networks must be very strong for 5G networks because they will be used to connect base stations to the core network. Because of the increased data speeds and lower latency needs of 5G, upgrading or developing this backhaul infrastructure is a significant issue. However, it must fulfill both of these criteria.

Consumption of Electricity:

Energy efficiency becomes a big concern as a result of the proliferation of connected devices and the rising energy consumption of 5G infrastructure. It is essential to decrease the amount of power that base stations and other network components consume in order to reduce both the negative impact on the environment and the costs of running the network.

Compatibility with Different Devices:

Not all currently available gadgets are suitable for use with 5G networks. Because of this incompatibility, users may have difficulties, since they may be required to upgrade their devices in order to make full use of the capabilities of 5G.

Challenges in Regulatory and Spectrum Areas

Allocation of the Spectrum:

Spectrum that is both ample and harmonized must be allotted in order for 5G networks to function properly. Every nation takes spectrum allotment in their own unique way, which might make it more difficult for countries around the world to communicate with one another. Coordination on an international level is necessary in order to guarantee that there will be sufficient spectrum for 5G.

Both interference and coordination are covered here.

The complicated regulatory task of coordinating the allocation of spectrum and reducing interference between different services and users operating in the same frequency bands is one that must be addressed. It is absolutely necessary to have efficient interference control in order to keep the high quality and dependability of 5G networks.

Concerns Regarding Health and Safety:

Concerns regarding potential health problems related with exposure to radio-frequency radiation have been aroused as a result of the deployment of 5G. In order to ensure the safe and responsible deployment of 5G networks, regulatory authorities need to address these concerns, conduct research, and establish safety guidelines.

Zoning and permitting on a local level:

In order to comply with local zoning restrictions and obtain the necessary licenses, the construction of small cells and base stations is frequently required. For network operators, navigating these regulatory processes can be a task that requires a significant investment of both time and money.

Challenges to Safety and Confidentiality

Security in cyberspace:

Cybersecurity is of the utmost importance in 5G networks due to the increased connectivity and potential attack surfaces that these networks provide. Protecting the network against malicious actors who are looking to exploit flaws and steal data is a difficult job.

Privacy of Information:

It is reasonable to be concerned about one's right to privacy in light of the fact that 5G networks would produce enormous amounts of data. The challenge of ensuring that personal and sensitive information is handled responsibly and securely is one that needs to be addressed by regulators as well as service providers.

Problems Facing the Economy

Expenses Related to Deployment

The deployment of 5G networks is an expensive endeavor, particularly in places with a high population density. The operators of networks are required to make investments in brand new infrastructure, spectrum licenses, and technological improvements. This investment presents a substantial obstacle, especially for those that operate on a smaller scale.

The yield on one's investment:

Due to the fact that the vast majority of 5G applications and services are still in their formative stages of development, generating a return on investment (ROI) through 5G networks might be a difficult task. It is possible that it will take some time for operators to receive a return on their investments that is beneficial.

The "Digital Divide":

There is a possibility that the deployment of 5G could make the digital gap worse because it might not be available to all populations, particularly in rural and underserved areas. This is one of the risks associated with the deployment of 5G. The bridging of this division is a challenge both economically and from a regulatory standpoint.

Problems Facing the Environment

In terms of energy consumption:

The amount of energy that will be consumed by 5G networks is a major cause for concern for the environment. To lessen the impact that 5G infrastructure has on the environment, it will be necessary to devise and put into practice methods and technologies that are more energy-efficient.

2.4 5G Use Cases and Applications

More than just a quicker internet connection, the fifth generation of wireless technology, often known as 5G, is a catalyst for dramatic change across many different industries and in day-to-day life. 5G has the ability to open a wide variety of use cases and applications that were previously impossible thanks to its much increased data speeds, ultra-low latency, and enhanced connectivity. In this piece, we'll take a look at some of the most exciting potential use cases and applications for 5G, which have the potential to radically alter the way we live our lives.

Improved Performance on Mobile Devices:

The fundamental goal behind the development of 5G was to create a superior mobile user experience. Users of mobile devices should anticipate a significant improvement in performance as a result of faster download and upload speeds, improved video streaming, and shorter response times for applications. This translates to an improved mobile gaming experience, high-quality video conferencing, and seamless media consumption, all of which can be done while on the move.

Revolution brought on by the Internet of Things (IoT)

The Internet of Things is poised to undergo a sea change as a result of 5G. It provides the connectivity that is necessary to support a large number of devices at the same time concurrently. As soon as 5G networks are able to effectively manage the expanding Internet of Things environment, the adoption of smart homes, cities, and industrial applications will skyrocket. 5G enables real-time communication and the interchange of data across Internet of Things devices. This includes anything from enhanced industrial automation to connected vehicles and smart thermostats.

Vehicles That Drive Themselves:

Communication systems that are dependable and have a low latency are essential for autonomous cars. Communication in real time between vehicles, infrastructure, and other users of the road is made possible by 5G networks, which helps to ensure that transportation is both safe and efficient. The automobile industry is about to undergo a revolutionary change as a result of this use case, which will make self-driving vehicles both safer and more efficient.

The Transformation of Healthcare:

The introduction of 5G will completely revolutionize the medical field. With 5G, medical practitioners will be able to execute sophisticated procedures remotely with very little lag time, which will make telemedicine and remote surgery more accessible. The technology also makes it possible to monitor patients in real time, which improves both the quality of medical care and the outcomes for patients.

Cities that are Smart:

5G is an essential component in the development of smart cities. It is beneficial for intelligent traffic management, monitoring of the environment, maintaining public safety, and increasing energy efficiency. Cities have the potential to become more environmentally friendly, connected, and responsive to the requirements of their citizens if they adopt 5G technology. Smart traffic signals, for instance, may make adjustments in real time to help alleviate traffic congestion, while air quality sensors can trigger alerts and interventions to help keep urban surroundings clean.

Instructional Technology and Distant Studying:

Education, including distance education, will become more immersive and interactive thanks to 5G. The use of augmented reality, remote access to educational resources, and virtual classrooms all contribute to increased productivity and interest in learning. This development in educational technology is particularly noteworthy in a society in which digital learning and distance education are becoming increasingly commonplace.

Agriculture with the Use of Precision Farming Techniques:

The collecting and analysis of data in real time is made possible by 5G, which enables precision agriculture. Farmers may monitor the conditions of the soil, the health of their crops, and the presence of insect infestations using IoT sensors and drones. This results in farming practices that are more effective and sustainable, which in turn leads to increased crop yields and decreased resource waste.

Production with the Fourth Industrial Revolution:

The rollout of 5G will be critical to the success of Industry 4.0, sometimes known as the fourth industrial revolution. The ultra-low latency and great dependability offered by 5G networks make it possible to perform remote monitoring and management of industrial machinery and procedures in real time. This results in increased automation, improved predictive maintenance, and higher levels of efficiency across a variety of industries, including manufacturing.

Entertainment with a Complete Immersion:

The entertainment business is going to be completely transformed by 5G. Applications that utilize augmented reality (AR) and virtual reality (VR) stand to gain a great deal from the low latency and high speed connectivity offered by 5G. Gameplay may become more involved and immersive for players, while content providers can provide their viewers with more satisfying augmented and virtual reality experiences.

Protection of the Public and Emergency Intervention:

5G has the potential to improve public safety by equipping first responders with data and communication capabilities that are updated in real time. This makes it possible to respond to disasters and emergencies in a more timely and effective manner. Emergencies present opportunities to make use of cutting-edge technologies like live video streaming in real time and monitoring carried out by drones.

Logistics, Supply Chain, and Procurement:

Supply chain management and logistics are both improved by the use of 5G thanks to its increased efficiency and accuracy. It is now feasible to implement real-time cargo tracking, driverless delivery trucks, and warehouse automation, all of which contribute to a reduction in operational expenses and an improvement of the supply chain experience as a whole.

The Provision of Power and Utilities:

By improving the efficiency of energy generation and delivery, the energy and utility sector stands to gain from the rollout of 5G. 5G will power smart grids, which will enable real-time monitoring and control. This will result in more effective management of energy resources, decreased waste, and enhanced dependability.

The fifth-generation wireless (5G) technology holds the potential to revolutionize how we live, work, and engage with the world around us. The use cases and applications of 5G are vast and diverse, ranging from the improvement of mobile experiences to the revolution of the internet of things (IoT), from the transformation of healthcare to the construction of smart cities.

It is reasonable to anticipate that as 5G networks continue to develop and mature, we will witness an acceleration of innovation across a variety of industries, an improvement in quality of life, and the appearance of new and exciting possibilities. To realize the full potential of this next-generation network, it is necessary for governments, corporations, and providers of technology to cooperate together and invest in 5G infrastructure.

Chapter 3

The Power of Cloud Computing

Computing on the cloud is quickly becoming recognized as one of the most revolutionary technologies of the 21st century. It signifies a fundamental change in the approach taken by individuals, businesses, and other organizations to the accessing, storing, and processing of data and applications. The power of the internet is harnessed by cloud computing so that a wide variety of services, including storage and processing, as well as machine learning and artificial intelligence, can be provided to users. Throughout this in-depth investigation, we look into the many facets of cloud computing's power, including its impact on a wide range of industries, the difficulties it presents, and the opportunities it presents for the future.

Computing in the Cloud: A Definition

1. **Public Cloud:** Services are provided to users via the internet, while the underlying hardware and software are owned and maintained by independent third-party providers. Users split the costs and resources involved.
2. **Private Cloud:** Services are utilized just by a single company, and the infrastructure may be located on or off the company's premises.
3. **Hybrid Cloud:** Combines public and private cloud computing, making it possible to share data and applications between the two types of clouds.

Key Attributes of Online Storage and Processing in the Cloud

1. **On-Demand Self-Service:** With this type of service, users are able to provision and manage resources on their own, without the involvement of a human from the service provider.
2. **Broad Network Access:** Services can be accessed from a diverse selection of devices and are made available via the internet.

3. **Resource Pooling:** In this model, resources are combined in order to service numerous clients at once. Users are relieved of the responsibility of being concerned about the underlying infrastructure.
4. **Rapid Elasticity:** Resources are able to be scaled up or down quickly and automatically in response to changes in demand.
5. **Measured Service:** The resources that are used for cloud computing are metered, which enables exact tracking and invoicing according to utilization.

The Advantages That Cloud Computing Can Offer to Businesses

1. **Savings Potential:** With cloud computing, businesses have less of a need to purchase and keep expensive on-premises infrastructure. This results in significant cost savings. This cost effectiveness is especially helpful for newly established startups and other small firms.
2. **Scalability:** Organizations are able to swiftly and efficiently scale up or down their information technology resources in response to changing workloads, which is especially beneficial for enterprises that experience workload fluctuations.
3. **Flexibility:** Cloud services provide users with access to a wide variety of applications and tools that may be customized to meet the requirements of individual businesses. Because of this flexibility, innovation and adaptation are encouraged.
4. **Global Reach:** The worldwide network of cloud service providers enables that companies can connect with customers all over the world without the need to invest in costly data centers located in numerous geographical areas.
5. Data Security and Backup Cloud service providers make significant investments in data security and backup, which makes it simpler for organizations to protect the data that is most important to them.

Influence on a Wide Range of Sectors

1. **Healthcare:** Cloud computing is transforming healthcare through the storing and exchange of patient data, telemedicine, and the creation of diagnostic and treatment tools. b. Financial Services: Cloud computing is reinventing financial services.
2. **Education:** Cloud-based e-learning platforms give students the ability to access instructional resources and collaborate with their classmates and teachers regardless of where they are located.
3. **The Government:** The government is a potential user of cloud computing, which might result in improved citizen services, data management, and disaster recovery.

4. **Finance:** The financial sector is heavily dependent on cloud computing for secure data
storage, the detection and prevention of fraud, and algorithmic trading.
5. **Amusement:** Streaming services and cloud gaming both depend on cloud infrastructure to deliver content and gaming experiences to audiences all over the world.
6. **Manufacturing:** Cloud computing is used in the manufacturing industry for preventative maintenance, the optimization of supply chains, and the improvement of production efficiencies.

Obstacles and Causes for Concern

The cloud computing model, despite offering enormous power and potential, is not without its share of issues and concerns.

1. **Data Security and Privacy risks:** Storing data off-site poses privacy and data security risks. Cloud service providers are obligated to protect their customers' data by using stringent security protocols.
2. **Downtime and Reliability:** When a company is dependent on cloud providers, any downtime or interruptions in service have the potential to negatively impact corporate operations. Service-level agreements, sometimes known as SLAs, are an indispensable tool for addressing this issue.
3. **Compliance and Regulation:** Different sectors of the economy and geographical areas have varying regulatory and compliance needs to meet. Cloud service providers have to successfully traverse this complicated ecosystem in order to guarantee that they satisfy all of the prerequisite criteria.
4. The costs associated with data transfer and bandwidth The process of uploading and downloading huge datasets can be time-consuming and costly. The costs involved need to be carefully considered by businesses.
5. Locking Users Into Their Provider's Cloud Moving data and applications from one cloud provider to another can be difficult and expensive. This lock-in can restrict the organization's ability to adapt to changing circumstances.

The Prospects for the Future of Cloud Computing

1. **Computing on the edge:** Cloud service providers are making their way toward the edge, which brings computing resources closer to the locations where data is generated. This is an extremely important consideration for low-latency applications such as driverless vehicles and the internet of things.
2. **Quantum Computing:** The power of quantum computing could have a tremendous impact on cloud computing, allowing for considerable advancements in encryption and data processing.

3. **Artificial Intelligence and Machine Learning:** Cloud platforms are increasingly combining capabilities for AI and machine learning, which offers new ways to evaluate and act on data.
4. **Green Computing:** Cloud service companies are looking into measures to lessen their negative influence on the environment, such as increasing the amount of renewable energy they use and how efficient their data centers are.
5. **Hybrid and Multi-Cloud settings:** It is quite likely that the future will consist of a combination of on-premises, private cloud, public cloud, and multi-cloud settings. One of the most important challenges and opportunities will be to effectively manage these ecosystems.

The advent of cloud computing has fundamentally altered the way in which we work and live. Its power to revolutionize impacts practically every part of our day-to-day existence, from the economic world and education to the medical field and entertainment, and everything in between. Even if problems and worries still exist, the cloud computing industry has a tremendous amount of room for growth in the years to come because to developments in areas such as edge computing, quantum computing, and artificial intelligence. Cloud computing will continue to be a driving force in the digital transformation of society as well as the economy on a global scale as technology continues to advance. In a world that is becoming increasingly data-driven and connected, it is crucial for individuals, businesses, and organizations to prosper by embracing the power of the cloud and successfully managing the obstacles it presents.

3.1 Introduction to Cloud Computing

The term "cloud computing" has evolved as a significant notion in the modern digital world, and its emergence has revolutionized the way in which businesses and individuals approach the storage, processing, and access of their data. This shift in paradigm has radically changed how ideas about information technology services are framed, how those services are delivered, and how those services are consumed. Cloud computing may be broken down into its most fundamental components, which include the delivery of computing services over the internet and the provision of easy, on-demand access to a shared pool of configurable computing resources. These resources can include networks, servers, storage, applications, and services. The purpose of this all-encompassing introduction is to delve into the fundamental components of cloud computing, including its history, important characteristics, deployment strategies, service models, and the profound consequences it has for a variety of businesses and society as a whole.

A Concise Historical Outline and Overview

The origins of cloud computing may be traced back to the 1960s, when J.C.R. Licklider introduced the idea of a "intergalactic computer network." This set the framework for the construction of ARPANET, which was the predecessor to the contemporary internet. However, the phrase "cloud computing" acquired major traction in the early 21st century when large-scale enterprises and technology giants began to harness the power of distributed computing to offer services through the internet. This is when the word "cloud computing" came into widespread use. Launched in 2006, Amazon Web Services (AWS) was a significant milestone, followed by the introduction of other prominent cloud service providers such as Google Cloud Platform and Microsoft Azure, which cemented the commercial feasibility and scalability of cloud computing. Amazon Web Services (AWS) was the first major cloud service provider.

Key Attributes of Online Storage and Processing in the Cloud

The term "cloud computing" refers to a type of online data storage and processing that differs significantly from more conventional computer approaches. Self-service on demand, access to a wide network, resource pooling, fast elasticity, and measurable service are a few examples of these capabilities. Users are able to provision computing capabilities such as server time and network storage through the use of on-demand self-service, which eliminates the need for human interaction with the service provider. Broad network access ensures that resources can be accessed using the network's conventional protocols and that the resources themselves are available through the network. The term "resource pooling" relates to the multi-tenant model, in which computing resources are pooled in order to service several users or tenants. Rapid elasticity makes it possible to scale resources in a smooth manner in order to suit shifting workloads. This ensures that both efficiency and performance are maximized. In addition, the idea of metered service makes it possible to have an accurate and open metering of resource utilization. This provides insight into the consumption of resources, which may be used for billing purposes as well as optimization.

Computing in the cloud: several deployment models

The deployment models for cloud computing include a variety of different configurations to satisfy the unique needs of different types of organizations. The public cloud, the private cloud, the hybrid cloud, and the community cloud are all examples of these models. The fact that public cloud services are delivered through the internet and are accessible to the entire population makes them an appealing choice for businesses that are looking for solutions that are both cost-effective and scalable. Private clouds, on the other hand, are limited to the use of a single company or organization. As a result, they offer a higher level of data and application control as well as protection. The benefits of public and private clouds are combined in hybrid clouds, which also enable data and applications to be transferred across the two types of clouds. Community clouds are cloud resources that are shared by multiple enterprises that have computing issues that are comparable to one another, such as compliance needs or security requirements.

The Different Types of Cloud Computing Services

The three basic service models that can be obtained through cloud computing are referred to as Infrastructure as a Service (IaaS), Platform as a Service (PaaS), and Software as a Service (SaaS). Users are able to construct their own information technology platforms by utilizing IaaS, which offers virtualized computing resources over the internet. These resources include virtual machines, storage, and networking. PaaS makes available to its users an environment in which they may design, run, and manage applications without having to deal with the complexities of constructing and maintaining the underlying infrastructure. The most popular type of service model, known as SaaS, delivers installed and operational software programs to customers via the internet on a subscription basis. This relieves customers of the responsibility of managing the underlying infrastructure.

The Consequences of Using Cloud Computing

The emergence of cloud computing has resulted in the release of a wide variety of consequences, which have the effect of transforming the dynamics of society, as well as the operations of businesses and information technologies. Computing in the cloud has simplified corporate processes, decreased the cost of infrastructure, and improved scalability. These benefits have helped organizations innovate and be more agile in the face of intense market competition. Small and medium-sized businesses, in particular, have reaped significant benefits from the cost-effectiveness and adaptability of cloud services, which have made it possible for them to compete on an even playing field with bigger businesses. In addition, cloud computing has helped pave the way for the development of a variety of cutting-edge technologies, such as the Internet of Things (IoT), artificial intelligence (AI), and big data analytics, which have all contributed to the acceleration of digital transformation across a wide range of industries. At the level of society, cloud computing has permitted remote work, worldwide cooperation, and better accessibility to information. This has promoted inclusion and connectedness across a wide range of demographics and geographical borders.

3.2 Cloud Services and Models

Cloud services have emerged as a revolutionary force in the ever-evolving environment of technology, and as a result, they have transformed the way in which individuals and organizations access and manage data and applications. Cloud services have had this effect because they allow users to store their data and applications remotely. The advent of cloud computing has resulted in a paradigm change, which has made it possible for businesses to become more adaptable, innovative, and cost-effective. It is vital, in order to comprehend the significance of cloud services, to investigate the several cloud models that are available and the advantages that they provide.

Cloud Models: A Variety of Imaginable Outcomes

Cloud computing comprises a variety of service models, each of which is tailored to meet a certain set of requirements and requirements. These approaches can generally be placed into one of three categories: software as a service (SaaS), platform as a service (PaaS), or infrastructure as a service (IaaS).

IaaS stands for "infrastructure as a service"

Infrastructure as a service, or IaaS, is the fundamental component of cloud services. It does this by making available over the internet a variety of virtualized computer resources, such as servers, storage, and networking. These resources can be provisioned and managed by users, who can also scale them up or down depending on their need. This flexibility is extremely beneficial to enterprises that experience varying workloads and have a requirement for the provisioning of infrastructure in a timely manner. Offerings of infrastructure as a service typically include well-known platforms such as Amazon Web Services (AWS), Microsoft Azure, and Google Cloud Platform (GCP).

IaaS offers a significant reduction in operating expenses, which is one of its primary benefits. Organizations pay just for the resources that they make use of as opposed to making capital investments in physical servers and data centers. Because it lowers both capital expenditures and operational costs, the pay-as-you-go model is an alternative that is appealing to companies of all sizes.

PaaS stands for "platform as a service"

PaaS is an extension of cloud computing that enables application developers to take advantage of a platform for the creation and deployment of their programs. With Platform as a Service (PaaS), developers are free to concentrate on the creation of apps rather than worrying about the underlying infrastructure. Because the platform handles the hardware, operating systems, and middleware, developers are free to focus on coding and coming up with innovative solutions. Heroku, Google App Engine, and Microsoft Azure App Service are three well-known examples of popular PaaS vendors.

The primary advantage of using PaaS is that it speeds up the process of developing applications. It encourages teamwork and collaboration among development teams and makes the development process more efficient overall. PaaS cuts down on the amount of time spent developing apps and enables a quicker time-to-market by abstracting the intricacies of infrastructure.

Software as a Service, sometimes known as "SaaS"

The Software as a Service (SaaS) model is the cloud model that places the most emphasis on the user. It makes computer programs available via the internet, where users can access them through a web browser or other application interface. Users need not worry about installing or maintaining the program; all they have to do is log in to begin utilizing it. Examples of popular software offered as a service include Google Workspace, Microsoft 365, and Salesforce.com.

One of the most notable benefits of SaaS is how convenient it is. It renders unnecessary the processes of installing software, keeping it updated, and performing maintenance, freeing businesses to concentrate on their fundamental activities. Users are freed from the responsibilities of IT management because SaaS providers take care of everything, from data backups to data security.

Advantages of Using Cloud Services

The advent of cloud services has ushered in a plethora of benefits that have fundamentally altered the way in which we work and live.

Scalability and flexibility: Cloud services give organizations the capacity to adjust the amount of resources they use in response to fluctuations in customer demand. This flexibility guarantees that businesses are able to successfully respond to the demands imposed by the business environment and changing market conditions. For example, a retail company can boost the capacity of its cloud resources to manage increased web traffic during the holiday shopping season, and then reduce those resources when the demand for their services diminishes.

Cloud services have the potential to drastically cut down on the costs of maintaining an IT infrastructure. It is no longer necessary for businesses to make costly investments in servers, data centers, and other forms of technology. Instead, they pay for the resources that they use, which makes it a cost-effective solution, particularly for new firms and smaller companies.

Accessibility and Collaborative Capabilities: With cloud computing, data and apps may be accessed from any location as long as there is an internet connection. Because more and more people are working from home these days, accessibility is more important than ever. Cloud-based collaboration solutions make it possible for teams to work together efficiently, despite the fact that they may be located in different locations.

Security and Reliability: The most reputable cloud service providers make significant financial investments in security protocols and data replication in order to guarantee the availability and integrity of their customers' data. It is not always within the financial means of individual organizations to provide such a high level of safety. The danger of data loss as a result of malfunctioning technology or natural disasters is significantly reduced when using cloud storage because the data is often backed up in many locations.

Cloud services enable businesses to develop and bring new products or services to market more quickly. These benefits are two of the many advantages that cloud computing offers. PaaS enables developers to rapidly design and deploy apps, while also allowing businesses to explore new markets and opportunities without being constrained by traditional infrastructure.

Concerns and Things to Take Into Account

Concerns About Privacy And Safety Storing data in the cloud can bring up questions about data privacy and safety. Potential dangers include data breaches and access by unauthorized parties. On the other hand, cloud service providers make significant investments in compliance and security requirements to reduce the likelihood of these dangers.

Costs Involved in Data Transfer and Bandwidth Utilization Moving significant volumes of data to and from the cloud may be a time-consuming and expensive process, especially for apps that need a lot of bandwidth. When it comes to establishing their cloud strategy, organizations need to take these costs into consideration.

Migration to the cloud may result in a situation known as vendor lock-in, in which an organization finds itself dependent on the ecosystem and tools offered by a particular cloud provider. It is absolutely necessary to think about the long-term repercussions of this lock-in and determine whether or not it is in line with the objectives of the organization.

Compliance and Data Governance: Various sectors of the economy and geographical areas have distinctly distinct requirements for compliance and data governance. Organizations are responsible for ensuring that the cloud provider they select can satisfy these standards and deliver the appropriate compliance certifications in order to continue using that provider.

Cloud computing, comprised of cloud services and models, has emerged as the primary impetus behind the digital transformation of both organizations and individuals' day-to-day life. The availability of computing resources, the capability to design apps, and the capability to use software all over the internet has transformed the way that we work, cooperate, and innovate.

As more and more businesses move their operations into the cloud, they will need to evaluate whether cloud model (IaaS, PaaS, or SaaS) will best meet their requirements while also taking into account the advantages and drawbacks of doing so. The flexibility, cost savings, and accessibility of cloud services are too attractive to resist; yet, a strategic approach to security, data governance, and vendor lock-in is required for a successful voyage into cloud computing.

The cloud has already played an essential part in the digital revolution, and its influence will only continue to grow as technology progresses, thereby opening up even more opportunities for companies as well as individuals. Cloud services will play an essential role in the digital future, whether it is to speed up innovation, simplify operations, or improve communication.

3.3 Benefits of Cloud Computing in Telecommunications

The industry of telecommunications is in the midst of a significant upheaval, which is being propelled by the rapid development of new technologies as well as the growing demand for increased connectivity. Cloud computing has emerged as a game-changer for telecommunications firms in this dynamic environment, delivering a wide range of benefits that boost efficiency, creativity, and customer experience. In this context, cloud computing has emerged as a game-changer for telecoms organizations. The tremendous benefits that cloud computing offers in the field of telecommunications are investigated throughout this essay.

1. **Capacity for Growth and Versatility**
   In the field of telecommunications, changing demand is common, especially in light of recent technological developments such as 5G and the Internet of

Things (IoT). Cloud computing gives telecommunications firms the ability to instantly scale up or down their resource allocation in response to shifting customer demands. The flexibility required to effectively satisfy these demands is provided by the cloud, and it is this flexibility that allows it to handle greater network traffic during peak hours as well as accommodate new services and technologies. Because of its scalability, the requirement for overprovisioning can be reduced, which results in cost savings and better usage of available resources.

2. **Effectiveness of the Budget**
   Investing a large amount of capital up front in data centers, servers, and networking equipment is required under traditional models of the infrastructure supporting telecommunications. Through the use of a pay-as-you-go model, which is made possible by cloud computing, this cost structure can be changed to one in which businesses only pay for the resources that they really use. This strategy decreases the amount of money spent on capital expenditures, which eases the financial pressure placed on telecom businesses. In addition, the cloud's centralized management makes upkeep and operational responsibilities much simpler, which further reduces the costs associated with upkeep and operation.
3. **NFV and SDN stand for "network function virtualization" and "software-defined networking," respectively**
   Two essential technologies in the telecommunications sector are software-defined networking (SDN) and network function virtualization (NFV), both of which are intricately linked to cloud computing. The replacement of discrete network appliances with virtualized network services that are hosted in the cloud is made possible by NFV for telecom operators. On the other side, software-defined networking (SDN) makes it possible to dynamically manage and optimize network resources.
   Cloud computing, network function virtualization (NFV), and software-defined networking (SDN) together create a robust platform for increased network agility and cost reduction. It makes it possible for telecommunications companies to speed up the process of launching new services, improve network performance, and simplify the management of physical network equipment.
4. **Immediate Deployment of Services**
   The process of building, testing, and deploying new services and applications can be streamlined with the help of cloud computing. Cloud platforms give telecommunications firms the ability to rapidly develop and launch new services, whether those services are new phone services, multimedia applications, or Internet of Things solutions. This adaptability is essential for maintaining one's position as a competitive player in a market where the rate of technological advancement is quickening.
5. **An Improved Experience for the Customer**
   In the field of telecommunications, cloud-based solutions are playing an essential

part in enhancing the overall consumer experience. Telecom companies are able to deliver more modern customer support services, such as chatbots and virtual assistants, because their contact centers are hosted on the cloud. These systems, which are powered by AI, are intended to manage client enquiries in an effective manner, hence lowering wait times and offering support around the clock.

In addition, cloud-based analytics and big data tools assist telecom businesses get insights into the behavior of their customers, which enables the companies to adjust their services and marketing tactics to the preferences of individual customers. Cloud computing makes it possible to perform tasks such as real-time service monitoring, personalized recommendation generation, and predictive maintenance.

6. **Geographic Reaches and Increasing Capabilities**

   There is frequently a need for telecommunications businesses to extend their service areas into new geographical areas or countries. The utilization of cloud computing makes the process of expanding network coverage much easier. Utilizing cloud providers that have data centers located all over the world is an alternative for businesses that would rather not start from scratch when constructing new data centers and infrastructure. This strategy quickens expansion while preserving the same level of dependability and performance throughout the process.

7. **Data Redundancy and Assurance of Data Integrity**

   In the field of telecommunications, maintaining data security and having several backups are absolutely necessary, as both disruptions in service and data breaches can have devastating effects. Cloud service providers make significant investments in a variety of security features, such as authentication, encryption, and access control. These precautions help to protect sensitive consumer data and ensure compliance with regulatory requirements.

   In addition to this, the infrastructure of the cloud is designed with redundancy in mind. Data is frequently distributed across numerous data centers, which lessens the likelihood that it may be lost as a result of catastrophic events or malfunctioning computer technology. When using traditional on-premises infrastructure, achieving this level of redundancy presents a number of challenges and a significant financial burden.

8. **Working Together and Creating New Things**

   The telecommunications business benefits from increased opportunities for collaboration and innovation thanks to cloud computing. By providing cloud-based platforms and application programming interfaces (APIs), telecom carriers can easily engage with technology partners, entrepreneurs, and developers. Because of this collaboration, new services and applications that are to the telecom company's and its customers' mutual benefit are more likely to be developed.

   In addition, cloud-based development environments and tools make it possible for telecom providers to swiftly experiment and invent new technologies. Companies are able to maintain their leadership position in a competitive industry by rapidly testing and releasing newly developed services.

9. **Positive Effects on the Environment**

One of the industries that is responsible for the greatest amount of energy use worldwide is the telecommunications sector. The ability of cloud computing to help telecom businesses streamline and improve their infrastructure is one way that cloud computing improves the environment. Traditional data centers are typically less friendly to the environment and more wasteful of energy than their cloud computing counterparts. This not only lowers the carbon footprint of the sector as a whole but also helps telecom businesses cut down on their operational expenses.

3.4 Cloud Security and Data Privacy

Computing in the cloud has evolved into a crucial component for the operation of a wide variety of companies and services in today's increasingly digital environment. The cloud has a lot of positive aspects, such as scalability and accessibility, but it also has a lot of negative aspects, such as serious security and data privacy problems. The protection of sensitive data and the maintenance of data privacy in cloud storage have recently emerged as two of the most pressing concerns for businesses and consumers alike. In this piece, we will discuss some of the most important components of cloud security as well as data privacy.

Acquiring Knowledge on Cloud Security

1. **A Model of Responsibility That Is Shared**
   The shared responsibility paradigm is an essential component of cloud computing security. It does this by dividing up the responsibilities between cloud users and cloud service providers (CSPs). CSPs are accountable for the protection of the cloud infrastructure, the protection of the physical environment, and certain aspects of the protection of the network. Users of the cloud, on the other hand, are the ones who are responsible for ensuring the safety of their data and apps while they are stored on the cloud.
   It is essential to have a solid understanding of this model since it outlines who is responsible for what, and companies need to execute security measures in accordance with this model. If you don't do it, you leave yourself open to weaknesses and the possibility of breaches.
2. **Management of Identities and Access Requests (IAM)**
   Identity and access management (IAM) is an essential component of cloud security. Access to cloud resources must be managed and controlled as part of this process. It is imperative for businesses to take the necessary precautions to guarantee that only authorized individuals can access sensitive data and apps. It is possible to protect against unwanted access by putting in place rigorous

authentication techniques, a role-based access control system, and constant monitoring.

3. **Codes and ciphers**
   Encryption of data is an essential component of any cloud-based security system. It protects the data both while it is being transmitted and while it is being stored. Data can be protected from illegal access or interception by using encryption both while it is at rest and while it is in transit. The encryption capabilities provided by a company's cloud service provider (CSP) should be understood by the organization, and further encryption should be implemented if appropriate.
4. **Security Surveillance and Responding to Incidents**
   The cloud's resources are regularly scanned for any signs of suspicious activity as part of the security monitoring process. Monitoring and analysis of logs and events in real time can be helpful in determining whether or not there have been any security breaches or suspicious activity. It is absolutely necessary to have a solid incident response plan in order to handle security issues in a timely manner, limit damage, and prevent further incidents from occurring.
5. **Obligations Regarding Conformity With Laws And Regulations**

Compliance and regulatory standards pertaining to the protection of personal information and data vary widely depending on both the sector and the geographic location. Users of cloud services are responsible for confirming that their cloud provider meets all of these requirements and possesses the appropriate certifications. For reasons of both data privacy and data security, compliance with standards such as GDPR, HIPAA, and SOC 2 is absolutely necessary.

The Cloud's Security Faces Obstacles

Location of the Data and Its Jurisdiction Because data that is kept in the cloud may live in numerous geographic areas, it can be challenging to keep track of and manage the data's jurisdiction. The fact that different nations have different rules and regulations pertaining to data privacy might make compliance efforts more difficult to achieve.

Data Access Control: Managing access control in an environment with several users and multiple devices can be a complicated process. The difficulty of limiting access to data to only the people who are permitted to view it is an ongoing one, particularly as businesses expand their operations.

Security of Data Transfer: Sending data to and from the cloud exposes it to potential vulnerabilities in terms of data security. It is essential to protect data while it is being transferred, but to do so effectively requires a solid understanding of encryption and secure communication protocols.

Acquiring Knowledge of Data Privacy

Consent: Individuals have the right to offer or withhold consent for the collection and processing of their data. Individuals also have the right to object to the collection and processing of their data. Before exploiting people's personal data, companies need to have their explicit and informed consent first.

Organizations have a responsibility to disclose all of their data collecting and usage policies, which constitutes transparency. The terms of service and privacy policies should be readily available to users and conveyed to them in a way that is understandable.

A fundamental idea of data privacy is known as "data minimization," which is collecting only the data that is required for a particular task and storing it for the very minimal amount of time necessary. It is important for organizations not to collect too much data or data that is not relevant.

The crucial nature of preventing unwanted access, breaches, and theft of personal data makes data security a top priority. It is essential to the protection of data privacy to implement stringent security measures, such as encryption, access restriction, and frequent security audits.

Confidentiality of Data Storing in the Cloud

Location of Data: Much to how cloud security can be affected by location, the privacy of data can also be affected by where it is physically stored. It is absolutely necessary to be aware of the physical location of data storage and processing in order to maintain compliance with data privacy legislation and to guarantee data sovereignty.

Organizations have a responsibility to ensure that they fully comprehend the terms and conditions imposed by their cloud service providers in reference to the ownership and control of their data. CSPs may, under some circumstances, assert rights over the data that is held on their respective platforms.

Processors of Data from Third Parties Cloud services frequently utilize the services of data processors from third parties. These processors should be thoroughly vetted by organizations to verify that they comply with all applicable data privacy standards and provide a sufficient level of security.

Best Practices for Protecting the Privacy and Integrity of Cloud Data

Evaluation of Cloud Service Providers It is important to thoroughly analyze cloud service providers based on their data privacy commitments, compliance certifications, and security policies.

Classification of Data: Group data into categories according to how sensitive it is, and then apply the proper security precautions to each group. The same level of security is not necessary for all of the data.

Encryption of Data: Make sure that data is encrypted both while it is being transferred and while it is being stored. To safeguard sensitive information, use encryption techniques with a high level of strength.

Access Control and Identity Management It is important to put in place reliable identity and access management solutions in order to properly manage user rights, responsibilities, and access.

Instruction in Security Awareness: Educate staff and users on the most effective methods for protecting data privacy and cloud security. One of the most common causes of data breaches is human mistake.

Conduct Routine Security Audits and Continuous Monitoring: In addition to conducting routine security audits, you should also continuously monitor cloud resources for any security flaws and threats.

Establishing Clear Policies and Procedures Regarding Data Privacy It is important to establish clear policies and procedures regarding data privacy that are in line with applicable rules and standards. Please ensure that these guidelines are reviewed on a regular basis and updated appropriately.

Protecting the digital landscape requires having strong measures in place for both the security of cloud storage and the privacy of user data. In order for businesses to protect their data and the privacy of their customers, they need to have a solid understanding of the shared responsibility model, have effective security measures in place, and comply with applicable data privacy rules. It is vital to keep alert and proactive in reducing risks and preserving trust in the cloud as cloud adoption continues to increase at a rapid rate. Security and privacy concerns will continue to be at the forefront of digital strategy as cloud adoption grows at a rapid rate.

Chapter 4

Convergence of 5G and Cloud

1. **The opening statement**

   A turning point in the development of digital technology has been reached with the confluence of 5G wireless networking and cloud computing. The fifth-generation mobile network (5G) and cloud computing are both revolutionary technologies in their own right; however, when coupled, they have the potential to radically alter the ways in which we connect to one another, communicate with one another, and compute. During this in-depth investigation, we will delve into the realms of fifth-generation (5G) wireless technology and cloud computing in order to gain a grasp of both the separate elements of these fields as well as the synergy that arises from the convergence of these fields.

2. **Acquiring Knowledge of the 5G Technology**

   2.1. What Is the 5G Network?

   In the field of wireless communication, the introduction of 5G, or the fifth generation of mobile network technology, represents a significant step forward. It guarantees increased data transfer speeds, a decrease in latency, and improved connectivity. In contrast to its predecessors, 5G is not simply an incremental enhancement; rather, it is a paradigm change that paves the way for a wide variety of new applications and use cases.

   2.2. Principal Attributes of 5G

   Enhanced Data Speeds: 5G delivers much faster data transmission rates, which makes it possible to stream high-definition videos, experience augmented reality (AR), and engage in virtual reality (VR) with very less buffering.

   Low Latency: The latency of 5G networks is expected to be lowered to milli-seconds, making them perfect for real-time applications such as remote surgery, driverless vehicles, and Internet of Things devices.

   Massive Connectivity Because 5G is capable of connecting a large number of devices at the same time, it is well suited for use in the Internet of Things (IoT) and in smart cities.

Network slicing is a feature that enables network operators to create virtual networks that are specifically tailored to the requirements of a variety of applications. This feature ensures that each application operates at its full potential.

Reliability: 5G networks are designed to be more dependable and stable than 4G networks, which will reduce the number of service interruptions and ensure that users have a consistent experience.

2.3. Applications of 5G Technology

5G makes real-time communication possible for autonomous vehicles, which enables these vehicles to make split-second judgments and function in a safe manner.

The low latency and great reliability offered by 5G networks are beneficial to telemedicine and other forms of remote healthcare delivery, such as teleconsultations and remote surgical procedures.

Smart Cities: 5G networks are vital for the implementation of smart city programs, providing support for services like as intelligent traffic control, public safety, and environmental monitoring.

Enhanced Mobile Experiences: 5G's ability to provide ultra-fast bandwidth and minimal latency makes mobile gaming, streaming, and augmented and virtual reality applications significantly better.

3. The Importance of Computing in the Cloud

3.1. What Exactly Is Computing on the Cloud?

The distribution of computing services through the use of the internet is made possible by a technology known as "cloud computing." Storage, computing power, databases, networking, software, and other services are included in this category of offerings. Computing in the cloud does away with the requirement that businesses have physical servers and data centers in operation. In addition, it provides a pay-as-you-go model, which makes it both cost-effective and scalable.

3.2. Principal Traits of Online Storage and Processing

Users are able to provision and manage computing resources on demand, without the need for human intervention from the service provider. This type of service is referred to as "on-demand self-service."

The term "broad network access" refers to the fact that cloud services can be accessed via the internet from a variety of devices and places.

Pooling of Resources: In order to satisfy the needs of a greater number of clients, cloud service providers pool their available resources. This results in more effective utilization of such resources.

Rapid elasticity denotes the ability to quickly scale up or down resource allocation in response to fluctuating demand.

Users are billed according to the real resources they consume, resulting in increased cost-effectiveness thanks to the measured service.

4. **The Confluence of Fifth-Generation Wireless and Cloud Computing**

4.1. The Infrastructure of the 5G Network

These data centers are responsible for processing and storing data as close to the end-users and devices as possible. There are two types of data centers: centralized and distributed.

Mobile Edge Computing (MEC) is a technique that moves cloud services to locations that are physically closer to the network's periphery, thereby cutting down on network latency and improving real-time processing capabilities.

Network Function Virtualization (NFV): NFV stands for "network function virtualization," and it permits the virtualization of network functions, making it possible for those functions to be deployed on cloud infrastructure.

Software-Defined Networking (SDN): SDN enables dynamic network administration and optimization, which increases the 5G network's degree of adaptability.

4.2. Computing on the Edge Within the 5G Ecosystem

Services with a Low Delay Edge computing enables applications such as autonomous vehicles, in which the ability to make decisions in real time is vital.

The low latency that is required for immersive augmented and virtual reality experiences can be provided via edge computing.

IoT: Edge computing is essential for Internet of Things devices since these devices require rapid data processing to guarantee real-time monitoring and control.

5. **The Advantages of Converging Together**

5.1. Increased Capacity and Speed of the Network

When the lightning-fast connectivity of 5G is combined with the cloud computing system's power to process enormous amounts of data, the resulting network achieves speeds and capacities that were previously inconceivable. Applications like high-definition streaming, virtual reality and augmented reality, and real-time gaming are all directly impacted by this.

5.2. Having a Low Latency

The decreased latency of 5G networks, which is further lowered by edge computing, enables real-time interactions, which in turn makes it possible to implement applications such as telemedicine, driverless vehicles, and industrial automation.

5.3. Capacity for Growth and Adaptability

Both fifth-generation mobile networks and cloud computing offer scalable infrastructure. The on-demand resources of the cloud and the network slicing capability of 5G give businesses the ability to easily adapt their networks and services to meet the requirements of individual customers.

5.4. An Enhanced Overall Experience for the User

The convergence assures a better user experience across a variety of applications and services, including faster downloads, seamless streaming, and improved augmented reality and virtual reality (AR/VR) experiences.

5.5. Assistance for Newly Emerged Technologies

Emerging technologies, such as artificial intelligence, machine learning, and the internet of things, rely heavily on the integration of cloud computing and 5G networks. It lays the groundwork upon which the development of these technologies can take place.

6. **Applications in the Industrial Sector**

The applications of the convergence of 5G and cloud computing are not restricted to a single sector; rather, they transcend several sectors and are revolutionizing the way in which we live, work, and communicate with one another.

6.1. Health and Safety

A few instances of how the convergence improves healthcare services are telemedicine, remote patient monitoring, and real-time medical imaging. Telemedicine, remote patient monitoring, and real-time medical imaging are just a few. It is now possible for medical professionals to deliver better care to patients and connect with them more effectively thanks to the combination of 5G technology and the cloud.

6.2. Intelligent Cities

Integrating data from a wide variety of sources and devices is essential to the functioning of a smart city. Together, 5G and the cloud make it feasible to gather, process, and analyze this data in real time, which enables smart traffic control, public safety, and energy efficiency, among other benefits.

6.3. Driverless Cars and Trucks

In order for autonomous vehicles to function properly, it is essential for 5G networks to have both low latency and high speed capabilities. These technologies make it possible for self-driving automobiles to engage in the rapid communication and decision-making that is necessary for safe navigation.

6.4. Games and Other Forms of Entertainment

The combination of 5G and the cloud presents enormous opportunities for advancement in the gaming sector. The lag that players feel is negligible, and the streaming quality is of a high standard, which enables cloud gaming and immersive VR experiences.

7. **Obstacles and Causes for Concern**

7.1. Safety and Personal Information

Emerging security risks are a direct result of the movement of data processing closer to network edges. It is essential to protect data both while it is in transit and while it is at the edge of the network in order to stop breaches. In addition, there is a possibility that edge computing will open up new attack avenues.

7.2. Costs of the Infrastructure

The establishment and upkeep of 5G infrastructure, including data centers and edge computing nodes, calls for significant financial investments. The anticipated benefits have to be greater than the costs in order to justify the costs.

7.3. Concerns Relating to Regulations and Policies

Challenges in terms of regulation and policy are presented as a result of the confluence of 5G and the cloud. The allotment of spectrum, data sovereignty rules, and privacy laws are all extremely important problems that need careful attention.

8. A Look Into The Future

The coming together of 5G wireless networks and cloud computing is not the destination of technical advancement but rather a significant step along the way. The following stage, which is frequently referred to as 6G, is already present in the thoughts of researchers and inventors. Connectivity, data processing, and overall user experiences are all projected to reach previously unimaginable heights as a result.

8.1. Sixth Generation and Beyond

Although 6G is still in its infancy stage, it is anticipated that it will build on the groundwork established by 5G and the cloud. It is possible that this will bring about technological developments such as terahertz frequencies and holographic communication, in addition to additional reductions in latency and increases in data transfer rates.

The coming together of fifth-generation wireless (5G) technology and cloud computing will bring about significant change in the field of technology. It ushers in a new era of connectedness, making possible applications and services that up until now existed only in the realm of science fiction. The convergence promises a digital future that will be more connected, efficient, and immersive if certain conditions are met. These conditions include enhanced network speed, reduced latency, and scalability. One industry that stands to benefit from the convergence is the entertainment industry.

Despite the fact that difficulties exist, technical progress and creativity continue to find solutions to them; as a result, the convergence of 5G and the cloud is becoming an important driving force in the evolution of our digital world.

4.1 How 5G and Cloud Technologies Complement Each Other

The convergence of fifth-generation wireless (5G) technology with cloud computing is transforming the way in which we connect to one another, interact with one another, and compute in today's rapidly advancing technological landscape. These two revolutionary technologies, while diverse in the benefits they provide, are progressively coming together to generate a synergy that promises benefits that cannot be matched by either one alone. In this investigation, we will investigate how the 5G network and cloud computing technologies may work together to open up new doors of opportunity and revolutionize existing business sectors.

1. **Acquiring Knowledge of the 5G Technology**

1.1. What Is the 5G Network?

In the realm of wireless communication, the advent of 5G, also known as the fifth generation of mobile network technology, represents a major step forward. In terms of speed, capacity, and capabilities, it represents a substantial departure from its predecessors, which are referred to as 4G and 3G, respectively.

1.2. The Principal Characteristics of 5G

Enhanced Data Speeds: 5G provides data transfer speeds that are substantially quicker than those of previous generations. This makes it possible to stream high-definition video, experience augmented reality (AR), and engage in virtual reality (VR) with very little buffering.

Extremely Low Latency: One of the defining characteristics of 5G is its extremely low latency, which reduces the amount of time it takes for data to travel from its point of origin to its final destination. This is absolutely necessary for applications that run in real time, such as telemedicine and driverless vehicles.

Massive Connectivity: 5G networks are designed to link a large number of devices at the same time, which makes it an excellent choice for the Internet of Things (IoT) and smart cities.

Slicing the Network: 5G enables the creation of virtual, specialized networks that can be tailored to the requirements of a variety of applications, ensuring that each will operate at its full potential.

Dependability: 5G networks have been developed to have enhanced dependability and stability, which will reduce the number of service interruptions and ensure a consistent user experience.

1.3. 5G's Potential Applications

5G makes real-time communication possible for autonomous vehicles, which enables these vehicles to make split-second judgments and function in a safe manner.

The low latency and great reliability offered by 5G networks are beneficial to telemedicine and other forms of remote healthcare delivery, such as teleconsultations and remote surgical procedures.

Smart Cities: 5G networks are vital for the implementation of smart city programs, providing support for services like as intelligent traffic control, public safety, and environmental monitoring.

Enhanced Mobile Experiences: 5G's ability to provide ultra-fast bandwidth and minimal latency makes mobile gaming, streaming, and augmented and virtual reality applications significantly better.

2. **The Importance of Computing in the Cloud**

   2.1. What Exactly Is Computing on the Cloud?

   The term "cloud computing" refers to a type of technology that uses the internet to provide a variety of computing services, such as data storage, processing power, databases, networking, and software, among other things. This move to the cloud reduces the need for enterprises to maintain physical servers and data centers, giving a pay-as-you-go model that is both cost-effective and scalable. Cloud computing is also known as internet-based computing or just cloud computing.

   2.2. Principal Traits of Online Storage and Processing

   Users are able to provision and manage computing resources on demand, without the need for human intervention from the service provider. This type of service is referred to as "on-demand self-service."

   The term "broad network access" refers to the fact that cloud services can be accessed via the internet from a variety of devices and places.

   Pooling of Resources: In order to satisfy the needs of a greater number of clients, cloud service providers pool their available resources. This results in more effective utilization of such resources.

   Rapid elasticity denotes the ability to quickly scale up or down resource allocation in response to fluctuating demand.

   Users are billed according to the real resources they consume, resulting in increased cost-effectiveness thanks to the measured service.

3. **The Convergence of Fifth-Generation Wireless and Cloud Computing**

   3.1 The Framework of the 5G Network Architecture

   Data Centers, Both Centralized and Distributed: These data centers are responsible for processing and storing data closer to end-users and devices, which reduces latency and improves the overall performance of the network.

   Mobile Edge Computing (MEC) is a technique that brings cloud computing resources to the edge of a network, therefore lowering network latency and opening the door to real-time data processing. This enables a more effective use of the resources provided by the network as well as apps that are more responsive.

   Network Function Virtualization (NFV) is a technology that enables the virtualization of network functions and makes it possible for those services to be implemented on cloud infrastructure. Because of this, the network is more versatile, it has a lower cost, and it is easier to manage.

   Software-Defined Networking (SDN): SDN enables dynamic network administration and optimization, which improves the overall user experience while also expanding the flexibility of 5G networks.

4. **How the 5G Network and Cloud Computing Can Complement One Another**

4.1 Increases in Both the Speed and Capacity of the Network

When the lightning-fast connectivity of 5G is combined with the cloud computing system's power to process enormous amounts of data, the resulting network achieves speeds and capacities that were previously inconceivable. Applications like high-definition streaming, virtual reality and augmented reality, and real-time gaming are all directly impacted by this.

4.2. Having a Low Latency

Real-time interactions are made possible by 5G networks' significantly decreased latency, which

is further lowered by edge computing, which is made possible by the cloud. This is absolutely necessary for applications such as telemedicine, autonomous vehicles, and industrial automation, all of which require instant decision-making.

4.3. Capacity for Growth and Adaptability

Both fifth-generation mobile networks and cloud computing offer scalable infrastructure. The on-demand resources of the cloud and the network slicing capability of 5G give businesses the ability to easily adapt their networks and services to meet the requirements of individual customers. This kind of adaptability is critical for a number of reasons, including the capacity to accommodate a sudden rise in the demand for data as well as the ability to optimize network resources for a specific application.

4.4. An Improved Overall Experience for the User

The convergence assures a better user experience across a variety of applications and services, including faster downloads, seamless streaming, and improved augmented reality and virtual reality (AR/VR) experiences. For instance, the lag that is typically experienced when streaming high-definition film or participating in online gaming is nearly erased, which results in activities that are more engaging and pleasurable.

4.5. Assistance for Newly Emerged Technologies

Emerging technologies are going to be built on a foundation that is formed by the combination of 5G and the cloud. Convergence of these technologies is necessary for the development of technologies like as artificial intelligence, machine learning, and the internet of things since it provides low latency, high connectivity speeds, and flexibility. These technologies significantly rely on the quick flow of data, real-time processing, and adaptability, all of which are made feasible by 5G and the cloud. Adaptability is especially important for the development of these technologies.

5. **Applications in the Industrial Sector**

5.1. Health Care Services

Telemedicine, remote patient monitoring, and real-time medical imaging are all made possible as a result of the convergence in the healthcare industry. It is now possible for medical professionals to deliver better care to patients and connect with them more effectively thanks to the combination of 5G technology and the cloud.

5.2. Intelligent Cities

Integrating data from a wide variety of sources and devices is essential to the functioning of a smart city. With 5G and the cloud, data can be collected, processed, and analyzed in real time, which can support a variety of applications including intelligent traffic management, public safety, and energy efficiency.

5.3. Driverless Cars and Trucks

In order for autonomous vehicles to function properly, it is essential for 5G networks to have both low latency and high speed capabilities. Additionally, edge computing must be supported by the cloud. These technologies make it possible for self-driving automobiles to engage in the rapid communication and decision-making that is necessary for safe navigation.

5.4. Gambling and Other Forms of Entertainment

The integration of 5G networks and cloud computing presents substantial opportunities for growth in the gaming and entertainment industries. The lag that players feel is negligible, and the streaming quality is of a high standard, which enables cloud gaming and immersive VR experiences.

6. **Obstacles and Causes for Concern**

6.1. Safety and Personal Information

New issues regarding data security are being raised as data processing advances closer to the network's edge. It is essential to protect data both while it is in transit and while it is at the edge of the network in order to stop breaches. In addition, there is a possibility that edge computing will offer new attack vectors, which must be protected against.

6.2. Costs of the Infrastructure

The establishment and upkeep of 5G infrastructure, including data centers and edge computing nodes, calls for significant financial investments. Although the benefits are substantial, the expenses have to be rationalized by reference to the anticipated returns.

6.3. Concerns Regarding Regulations and Policies

Challenges in terms of regulation and policy are presented as a result of the confluence of 5G and the cloud. Data sovereignty, privacy rules, and the distribution of spectrum are all important concerns that demand careful analysis and collaboration from governments, businesses, and the companies that provide technology.

7. **A Look Into the Future**

The coming together of fifth-generation wireless networks with cloud computing is not the pinnacle of technological advancement but rather an important step along the way. The following stage, which is frequently referred to as 6G, is already present in the thoughts of researchers and inventors. It is anticipated that it will expand upon the foundation laid by 5G and the cloud, propelling connection, data processing, and user experiences to even higher heights than they currently are.

7.1. Beyond 6G in Acceleration

Even though 6G technology is in its infancy, it is anticipated that it will continue the general trend of technological advancement. It is possible that this will bring about technological developments such as terahertz frequencies and holographic communication, in addition to additional reductions in latency and increases in data transfer rates. This will usher in a future that is even more connected and intelligent than we could have ever imagined, opening up new possibilities for invention and networking.

The coming together of fifth-generation wireless (5G) technology and cloud computing will bring about significant change in the field of technology. It ushers in a new era of connectedness, making possible applications and services that up until now existed only in the realm of science fiction. These two technologies have a number of properties that are complementary to one another. These features include speed and low latency, as well as scalability and adaptability. Together, these features open up a universe of possibilities that transcend numerous industries and improve the way in which we live, work, and interact with one another. Despite the fact that difficulties exist, technical progress and creativity continue to find solutions to them; as a result, the convergence of 5G and the cloud is becoming an important driving force in the evolution of our digital world. As we stand on the precipice of a future that is more interconnected, intelligent, and promising than it has ever been, it is a monument to the limitless potential of human creativity.

4.2 The Role of Edge Computing in the Convergence

A new era of connectivity and innovation is about to begin as a result of the confluence of 5G and cloud technologies, which has taken center stage as the digital landscape continues to shift and develop. Computing at the edge of networks is one of the key factors that will determine the direction that technology will go in the future.

Edge computing is a crucial component in this game-changing synergy because it enables computer resources to be placed in greater proximity to the locations where data and applications are generated. In the course of this in-depth investigation, we look into the function that edge computing plays in the coming together of 5G and cloud technologies.

1. **Exactly what does "Edge Computing" mean?**
   Instead than depending on a centralized cloud or data center, edge computing is a concept of decentralized computing that places computational power and data storage closer to the location where it is needed. As the need for real-time processing, low latency, and data privacy continues to increase, it has become vital to make this shift to the "edge" of the network.

2. **The Principal Traits of an Edge Computing Environment**

   It is crucial to look at the major aspects of edge computing in order to have an understanding of the function that it plays in the convergence of 5G and cloud technologies.

   2.1 Extremely Low Latencies

   By processing data much closer to its original source, edge computing drastically minimizes the amount of time spent waiting for results. This is of the utmost importance for applications such as industrial automation, augmented and virtual reality, and self-driving vehicles, all of which require decisions to be made in real time.

   2.2. Processing of Data Directly at the Source

   Because data is handled locally using edge computing, there is less of a need to send massive volumes of data to centralized data centers. This is a significant benefit. By doing so, bandwidth is conserved, and delays in the transfer of data are reduced.

   2.3. Capacity to Grow

   Edge computing enables the distribution of computing resources across a network at a variety of different locations. Scalability is improved as a result of this since resources can be directed to where they are most needed.

   2.4. Redundancy and reliability

   Computing at the edge has the potential to improve the redundancy and reliability of a system. In the event that an edge device or node fails to function, the system will be able to continue functioning normally thanks to the adjacent edge resources.

3. **The Importance of Computing at the Periphery in the Convergence**

   3.1. Lessening the Amount of Delay

   The elimination of latency is the most important contribution that edge computing makes to the overall process of convergence. Edge computing takes low-latency connectivity one step farther than what is offered by 5G networks, which currently provide it. Edge computing supports applications that require real-time responses, such as driverless vehicles, telemedicine, and industrial automation. This is accomplished by processing data closer to the source than traditional methods. It guarantees that data is acted upon nearly instantly, which is crucial for the success of these apps since it ensures that data is acted upon very instantly.

   3.2. Improving Real-Time Processing

   Computing at the network's edge enables the processing of data in real time. This is known as edge computing. Applications that demand fast decision-making and responses absolutely need this real-time capacity in order to function properly. For instance, in order for autonomous vehicles to make instantaneous decisions regarding driving, the data from its sensors needs to be processed locally. Monitoring of vital signs in real time by telemedicine has the potential to save lives. Through the use of edge computing, these vital apps will continue to operate faultlessly and with a small amount of lag.

3.3. Decentralizing Resources from the Central Cloud

The combination of 5G with edge computing enables some jobs and processing to be moved from central cloud resources to edge devices and nodes, which frees up those cloud resources for other uses. This lightens the stress on the central cloud infrastructure, which in turn makes it more effective and decreases the associated costs. In addition to this, it lessens the quantity of data that needs to be sent to the cloud for processing, which in turn helps save bandwidth on the network.

3.4 Providing Support for the Internet of Things and Smart Devices

The Internet of Things (IoT) and other types of smart devices are made possible by edge computing in a fundamental way. IoT devices that call for low-latency data processing are made easier to deploy because to the convergence of 5G wireless networking, cloud computing, and edge computing. These gadgets are becoming more and more interwoven into various facets of our life, ranging from applications for the industrial internet of things to smart homes.

3.5. Making It Possible to Provide Location-Based Services

Computing at the edge provides location-based services, which deliver individualized content or services to users based on their current location in the world. For instance, retail organizations can employ edge computing to provide customers within their stores with location-specific marketing or assistance with navigation by using services such as Google Maps.

4. **Applications of Edge Computing in Industry for the Convergence**

4.1. The Healthcare System

Edge computing is having a profound impact on the healthcare industry by making it possible to perform remote patient monitoring and telemedicine. No matter where a patient is located, medical practitioners may monitor their vital signs and give urgent care because to the ability to process medical data locally and in real time.

4.2. Intelligent Cities

Edge computing is essential for smart city programs because it enables the processing of data from sensors, cameras, and other Internet of Things devices in real time. The collection and analysis of this data helps cities become better at managing traffic, ensuring public safety, monitoring the environment, and becoming more energy efficient.

4.3. Automation in the Industrial Sector

Computing at the network's edge plays a critical part in the optimization of operations in industrial settings. It makes possible the monitoring and management of production equipment in real time, which is essential for ensuring that operational efficiency is maintained and that downtime is kept to a minimum.

4.4. Driverless Cars and Trucks

Computing at the network's edge is vital to the development of successful autonomous cars. For these vehicles to be capable of making split-second decisions regarding driving and passenger safety, the processing of sensor data must occur instantaneously.

4.5. Games and Other Forms of Entertainment

Through the reduction of latency and the facilitation of cloud gaming services, edge computing contributes to an improvement in the gaming and entertainment industries. Experiences of low-latency, high-quality online gaming, as well as content that is immersive in virtual reality, are available to gamers.

5. **Obstacles and Causes for Concern**

5.1. Protection

Concerns regarding data safety are raised as a result of the decentralized nature of edge computing. There is a possibility that edge devices and nodes are more susceptible to both cyberattacks and physical interference. The safety of sensitive data and the protection of the infrastructure at the edge of the network are of the utmost importance.

5.2. Management of the Data

Because computational resources are distributed at the edge, there is a need for efficient data management solutions. The consistency, integrity, and accessibility of data must be monitored and maintained across all edge devices by organizations.

5.3. Capacity to Grow

The capacity to scale near the edge is a difficult endeavor. In order to keep the network's performance at an optimal level while managing a diverse set of edge devices and nodes, effective resource allocation and orchestration are required.

5.4. Standardization and interoperability

Establishing standards and interoperability between various edge devices and platforms is necessary in order to make full use of the potential that can be unlocked by edge computing. This guarantees that the integration is smooth and the activities are efficient.

6. **A Look Into The Future**

The function of edge computing in the convergence of 5G and cloud technologies is expected to assume an increasingly important role in the not-too-distant future. Edge computing will play an essential part in the support of upcoming technologies such as 6G, AI, and the Internet of Things as technology continues to progress at a rapid pace. It will continue to promote innovation across a wide range of industries by providing low-latency, real-time processing capabilities, which are critical for applications of the next generation.

Edge computing is a key component in the convergence of 5G and cloud technologies. It enables low-latency, real-time processing and provides support for a wide variety of applications in a variety of industries. Edge computing will play a vital role in creating the future of technology, connecting us in ways that were once only imagined in science fiction. This role will become more important as the digital landscape continues to grow.

Despite the fact that there are obstacles to overcome, innovations and developments in security and data management will further increase the role that edge computing plays in the convergence. This will move us closer to a digital future that is more connected, efficient, and intelligent.

4.3 Building the Infrastructure for Synergy

The convergence of 5G and cloud technologies is transforming the way in which we connect to one another, interact with one another, and compute in the ever-changing world of technology. This convergence carries with it the promise of unmatched benefits; nevertheless, the actualization of those benefits is contingent on the construction of a solid infrastructure that is able to facilitate this synergy. As part of this in-depth investigation, we look into the process of constructing the infrastructure for 5G and cloud technologies to work in tandem with one another.

1. **Acquiring an Understanding of How 5G and Cloud Technologies Are Converging**

   Before going into the infrastructure, it is vital to understand the relevance of the confluence of

   5G and cloud technologies. This should be done before beginning the infrastructure design process.

   5G, or the fifth generation of mobile network technology, is a major step forward for wireless communication. 5G is the fifth generation of mobile network technology. It provides more capacity, decreased latency, and quicker data speeds, paving the way for new applications and use cases.

   Cloud computing is a method of providing computer services through the use of the internet. These services include storage, processing power, databases, and a great deal more. It provides businesses with a model that is both scalable and cost-effective, as it eliminates the need for the businesses to maintain their own physical servers and data centers.

   The convergence of 5G and cloud technologies is a strategic pairing because one technology complements the other in many ways, resulting in greater network performance, low latency, scalability, and improved user experiences. This strategic coupling was made possible as a result of the convergence of these two technologies. Nevertheless, in order to take use of these benefits, a robust infrastructure is required.

2. Establishing a Foundation for Synergy by Building Its Infrastructure

2.1. The Architecture of the Network

This convergence revolves mostly around the design of the underlying networks. It entails the installation of 5G base stations in addition to network core components. Both centralized cloud data centers and dispersed edge computing nodes need to be supported by the infrastructure, therefore it must be designed accordingly. In addition to that, it includes the incorporation of software-defined networking (SDN) and network function virtualization (NFV), all of which work together to make network administration more fluid and adaptable.

2.2. Computing at the Periphery and Data Centers

It is necessary for the infrastructure to have data centers that are placed in such a way as to take full advantage of their ability to meet the low-latency requirements of 5G applications. This comprises edge computing facilities for real-time processing at the network's periphery as well as centralized data centers for handling tasks that can be done using a cloud model that is more familiar to most people. In order to lessen the impact of latency on applications like driverless vehicles and augmented reality, edge computing is an extremely important factor to consider.

2.3. Slicing of the Network

The slicing of networks is an essential part of the process of developing infrastructure for synergy. It makes it possible to create virtual networks inside of a physical network that is already in use. It is possible to tailor each slice to the specifications demanded by a particular application, whether that application requires a high bandwidth, low latency, or assured level of reliability. This strategy enhances the performance of network resources across a variety of use cases.

2.4. The Frequency Spectrum at High Levels

5G is dependent on high-frequency spectrum bands, which are necessary in order to achieve the promised data throughput and low latency levels. The deployment of these high-frequency antennas and radio equipment is an essential component of the infrastructure and must be included.

2.5. Protective Steps to Take

The most important thing is to have a secure infrastructure. Because data processing is moving closer to the edge of the network, additional safety precautions are required to secure any sensitive information that may be there. This contains highly effective techniques for monitoring, authentication, and data encryption.

2.6. Management of the Data

It is essential to have effective data management in order to ensure that data is processed and sent to the appropriate locations. The data routing, storage, and retrieval technologies that are included in this architecture have been fine-tuned to meet the requirements of 5G and cloud applications.

3. **Obstacles Encountered When Constructing the Synergy-Enabling Infrastructure**

3.1. Exorbitant Fees

Putting in place infrastructure for 5G, data centers in the cloud, and edge computing facilities all represent considerable investments. The predicted benefits, which include improved user experiences, operational savings, and new income prospects, need to be sufficient to justify these costs.

3.2 Obstacles Created by Regulations and Policies

The deployment of infrastructure for 5G networks frequently runs into problems with regulations and policies. The rate at which infrastructure is developed and whether or not it can be built at all can both be impacted by factors such as spectrum allotment, data privacy, and local zoning rules.

3.3. Concerns Regarding Safety and Confidentiality

As data processing moves closer to the edge of the network, new concerns regarding privacy and security are brought to the forefront. In order to prevent breaches and the loss of data, it is essential to ensure the security of the data and the edge computing nodes.

3.4. Operational Compatibility

It can be difficult to ensure interoperability across the many 5G and cloud components that come from a variety of different manufacturers. In order to facilitate seamless integration, a consistent approach to interfaces and technology is very necessary.

3.5. Scalability and adaptability

The infrastructure needs to be constructed so that it can scale up easily and adjust to new circumstances easily. It should be able to accommodate increased data demands and the incorporation of future technologies without necessitating a major rewrite of the system.

4. **The Part Played by Business and the Government**

4.1. The Private Industry

Building and maintaining the infrastructure is mostly the responsibility of technology manufacturers, cloud service providers, and organizations that provide telecommunications services. They are investing in the creation of data centers, edge computing facilities, and 5G networks. Their creativity is the primary force behind the progression of this confluence.

4.2. Administration

The legal framework and spectrum allocation that are required for the implementation of 5G infrastructure are both provided by national governments. They also have the ability to provide financial incentives and subsidies in order to encourage private sector investment in these technologies. When it comes to promoting an atmosphere that is conducive to technological innovation and safeguarding the safety and privacy of these networks, governmental agencies play a pivotal role in both of these areas.

5. **The Advantages of Having a Converged Infrastructure**

5.1. An Enhanced Overall Feeling for the User

Users will enjoy improved experiences with applications like as streaming media, video gaming, and augmented reality as a result of higher data rates, decreased latency, and seamless connectivity.

5.2. Facilitating the Development of Innovative Applications

Innovative applications in a variety of fields, including healthcare, smart cities, autonomous vehicles, and more are supported by the converged infrastructure. Just a few examples are autonomous driving that is both safe and efficient, real-time telemedicine, and better traffic management.

5.3. Effectiveness of the Operations

As a result of the convergence, businesses will see increased operational efficiency. The integration of cloud computing with 5G networks makes the processing of data more efficient and shortens the amount of time needed to make essential decisions.

5.4. Brand-New Prospects for Commercial Enterprise

The infrastructure opens up new avenues for commercial activity, such as edge computing services and Internet of Things applications. These technologies make it possible for a variety of industries to generate cash.

5.5. Recent Developments in Technology

The infrastructure enables new technologies such as artificial intelligence (AI), machine learning, and the Internet of Things (IoT) by supplying the connectivity and data processing capabilities that are necessary for these technologies.

6. **A Look Into The Future**

The infrastructure necessary to facilitate the synergy between 5G and cloud technologies is still undergoing constant development. This infrastructure will need to adapt and develop as technology continues to advance and as increased demands are placed on it for faster data rates, lower latency, and real-time processing.

There is also the possibility that the future could offer the promise of 6G technology, which will expand upon the groundwork established by 5G and cloud computing. In the near future, terahertz frequencies, holographic communication, and even more remarkable data speeds and reduced latency are on the horizon, all of which will further advance the possibilities presented by this confluence.

The combination of 5G and cloud technologies offers tremendous promise, but the actualization of that promise is contingent on the creation of an infrastructure that is both robust and flexible. This infrastructure is the backbone that enables faster data rates, lower latency, real-time processing, and improved user experiences. Those four things are all made possible by real-time processing. It bolsters the development of creative applications, opens doors to new commercial opportunities, and propels the growth of technology.

In spite of the fact that obstacles exist, it is absolutely necessary for the private sector and the

government to work together in order to overcome them. The infrastructure enabling the synergy between 5G and cloud technologies will continue to be a dynamic and vital component of our technological future, linking us in ways that were once only imagined in science fiction. This will be the case even as the digital landscape continues to undergo change.

Chapter 5

Transforming Industries with 5G and Cloud

The coming together of 5G and cloud technologies signifies a seismic change in the world of technology. This convergence holds the potential to transform whole industries, redefine the way we work and communicate, and propel creativity to new heights. In this in-depth investigation, we look into the multiple ways in which 5G and the cloud are altering several industries, such as healthcare and manufacturing, as well as agriculture and smart cities. This convergence is more than just an improvement in technology; rather, it is a driver of change and progress across the board.

1. **Acquiring an Understanding of How 5G and Cloud Technologies Are Converging**

   1.1. Technology Based on 5G

   Enhanced Data Speeds: 5G delivers data transfer speeds that are substantially faster than its predecessors, making it possible to stream high-definition video, experience augmented reality (AR), and engage in virtual reality (VR) with very no buffering.

   Extremely Low Latency: The 5G network is planned to offer extremely low latency, which will cut down on the amount of time it takes for data to travel from its origin to its destination. This is absolutely necessary for applications that run in real time, including driverless vehicles and telemedicine.

   Massive Connectivity: Because 5G networks are capable of connecting a large number of devices at the same time, they are ideally suited for the Internet of Things (IoT) as well as smart cities.

   Slicing the Network: 5G enables the creation of virtual, specialized networks that can be tailored to the requirements of a variety of applications, ensuring that each will operate at its full potential.

   Dependability: 5G networks have been developed to have enhanced dependability and stability, which will reduce the number of service interruptions and ensure a consistent user experience.

1.2. Technologies Hosted in the Cloud

The term "cloud computing" refers to the delivery of computer services, such as storage, processing power, databases, networking, and software, via the internet. This move to the cloud reduces the need for enterprises to maintain physical servers and data centers, giving a pay-as-you-go model that is both cost-effective and scalable. Cloud computing is also known as internet-based computing or just cloud computing.

2. How the Fifth Generation Mobile Network and Cloud Technologies Will Revolutionize Industries

2.1. The Healthcare System

2.1.1 Telemedicine and the Monitoring of Patients from a Remote Location

Telemedicine and other forms of remote patient monitoring are now significantly easier to implement because to recent advancements in cloud computing and 5G networking. The use of high-quality video conferencing, monitoring of patients' health data in real time, and consultations conducted remotely are becoming the standard. Patients are able to obtain medical care without leaving the convenience of their own homes, which eases the strain placed on healthcare institutions while also expanding patients' access to care.

2.1.2. Enhancements to the Diagnostic Procedures and Imaging

Imaging techniques used in medicine, such as MRI and CT scans, produce significant amounts of data. This data can be instantly transmitted and analysed thanks to the capabilities of 5G and cloud computing, leading to quicker diagnostics and decisions on treatment that are made more promptly. Additionally, more advanced imaging techniques such as augmented reality-assisted surgery and three-dimensional visualization are becoming increasingly practicable.

2.1.3. Improved Methods of Drug Discovery

In the pharmaceutical industry, the use of 5G and cloud computing can facilitate the analysis of huge datasets and the execution of complicated simulations. This speeds up the process of discovering novel drugs, which could eventually lead to the creation of new treatments for a variety of disorders.

2.2. Intelligent Cities

2.2.1. Managing Traffic and Providing Transportation

For the purpose of improving traffic flow, intelligent traffic management systems collect data in real time from sensors and cameras that are connected to 5G networks. The processing of this data on the cloud enables analytics to cut down on traffic congestion, shorten travel times, and improve overall road safety.

2.2.2 Environmental Watching and Reporting

The air quality, pollution levels, and weather conditions in a city can be monitored using sensors that are equipped with 5G technology. The processing of this data takes place on the cloud in order to facilitate environmental management and efforts relating to sustainability.

2.2.3. Safety of the Public

5G is being used by public safety organizations to decrease response times and improve incident management. Communication in real time, video surveillance, and data analysis performed in the cloud are three of the instruments that offer law enforcement and emergency services with the capabilities necessary to keep cities safe.

2.3. Production and the Fourth Industrial Revolution

2.3.1 Automation and the Internet of Things in Industry

Industrial Internet of Things (IIoT) solutions are becoming increasingly popular among manufacturers as a means to boost operational efficiency and cut downtime. Real-time data transmission is made possible by 5G connectivity, which, in conjunction with cloud-based analytics, helps improve predictive maintenance and automation.

2.3.2 The Management of the Supply Chain

The management of supply chains is becoming more agile and responsive as a result of technological advancements such as 5G and cloud computing. These technological innovations enable better decision-making and reduce supply chain interruptions by providing real-time visibility into inventory, logistics, and demand.

2.3.3 Quality Assurance and On-Site and Off-Site Inspections

For the purposes of quality control and remote inspections, manufacturers are increasingly turning to high-resolution cameras and sensors that are connected to 5G networks. This ensures that goods meet high standards and allows specialists to remotely assess manufacturing processes, avoiding the need for on-site inspections to the manufacturing facility.

2.4. Self-Driving Cars and Trucks

The revolutionary force of 5G and cloud convergence is best illustrated by autonomous vehicles (AVs), often known as driverless cars.

2.4.1 Communication in Real Time

In order to operate without risk, AVs require communication systems with extremely low latency. 5G networks enable instant communication, which is necessary for autonomous vehicles to traverse challenging road conditions and make judgments in the moment.

2.4.2 Computing at the Edge

Edge computing, which is made feasible by cloud computing, enables autonomous vehicles to process data locally, which reduces the need to send vast volumes of data to remote data centers. Because of this local processing, AVs are able to react quickly to a variety of changing circumstances.

2.4.3 Improvements to the Navigation System and Safety

5G and cloud technology are utilized by AVs to generate high-definition maps and to provide real-time updates. This not only improves navigation, but it also increases safety because it can recognize and respond to threats more quickly than human drivers.

2.5 Recreational Activities and Amusements

2.5.1 Online Gaming in the Cloud

The proliferation of cloud gaming services enables gamers to play games streamed over 5G networks with minimum interruptions in gameplay. This paves the way for gamers to have access to high-quality gaming experiences on a wide variety of devices, independent of the capabilities of the underlying hardware.

2.5.2. Augmented Reality and Virtual Reality

The 5G network and cloud computing have made important contributions to the improvement of virtual reality (VR) and augmented reality (AR) experiences. Users are able to access content and applications that are immersive without experiencing any latency, which enables a new degree of involvement and immersion.

2.5.3 Streaming Video of High Quality

The convergence has also led to improvements in video streaming services, which now provide content in high definition with significantly reduced buffering times. Both those who create content and those who consume it will gain from this development.

2.6. Agricultural Production

2.6.1 The Application of Precision Agriculture

Farmers are use drones and sensors that are connected to 5G networks to monitor the status of their crops, as well as the quality of the soil and the weather. Cloud-based analytics provide information that can be used for precision agriculture, with the goals of boosting yields and optimizing resource use.

2.6.2. Monitoring of the Livestock

Wearable gadgets that monitor the health and location of animals can now be used in conjunction with 5G networks to facilitate livestock monitoring. Both the well-being of animals and the management of farms are improved as a result of this.

2.6.3 Transparency Within the Supply Chain

Consumers are able to acquire greater understanding of the provenance of agricultural products

by accessing real-time data from sensors connected to 5G networks and the cloud. This transparency is essential for both the safety of the food and its ability to be traced.

3. **Obstacles and Things to Take Into Account**

3.1. Safety and Personal Information

The increased connectedness and capability for processing data may give rise to worries over data privacy and security. The protection of sensitive information and the maintenance of data privacy are of the utmost importance.

3.2. Investments in Physical Infrastructure

The construction and upkeep of the infrastructure required to enable 5G and cloud technologies represents a large financial expenditure. Because of this, co-operation between the private sector and the government is required in order to guarantee the availability of the necessary resources and regulatory framework.

3.3. Operational Compatibility

Establishing standards and interoperability between various technologies and providers is necessary in order to make the most of the opportunities presented by convergence. This ensures that the different systems may function together without any problems.

3.4 Competencies and the Workforce

A workforce with the necessary skills is required if we are going to realize the full potential of these technologies. For individuals to be able to work with 5G and cloud technologies, there must first be established training and education programs that provide people with the necessary knowledge and abilities.

3.5. The Impact on the Environment

The growing application of technology across a variety of sectors must to be done so with consideration for its effects on the natural world. The solutions should have as their primary focus the reduction of carbon footprints and the promotion of sustainable practices.

4. **A Look Into The Future**

The coming together of 5G and cloud technologies is not the end of the road, but rather a significant landmark along the path of ongoing technological progress. Emerging technologies such as sixth-generation wireless (6G), artificial intelligence (AI), and the Internet of Things (IoT) will continue to push the limits of what is now achievable.

4.1. Sixth Generation and Beyond

There are numerous signs pointing to the imminent arrival of 6G technology. Although it is still in its early phases, it is anticipated that it will expand upon the foundation laid by technologies such as 5G and the cloud. It's possible that 6G may usher in innovations like terahertz frequencies and holographic communication, in addition to even more astounding data transfer speeds and reduced latency.

5. **The inference drawn**

There has been a significant shift in the direction that the world of technology is heading as a result of the convergence of 5G and cloud technologies. It has the ability to revolutionize entire industries, raise standards of living across the board, and propel innovation to previously unimaginable heights. The capacity to access real-time data, communicate with a low amount of delay, and scale one's computing resources offers up a virtually infinite number of options.

Despite the fact that there are obstacles to overcome, technical progress and innovation are consistently finding ways to do so, which is what makes the convergence of 5G and the cloud such a transformational force.

As we are on the brink of a future that is more connected, efficient, and intelligent than ever before, it is a monument to the limitless potential of human creativity that we have reached this point. Industries who are willing to adopt these technologies will be in a position to benefit from opportunities and capabilities that have never been seen before in the future.

5.1 Healthcare and Telemedicine

The development of telemedicine, a subfield of telehealth that makes remote diagnosis and treatment possible, is having a tremendous effect on the current state of the healthcare system, which is experiencing a fundamental transition. The application of technology, most notably telemedicine, is reshaping the manner in which healthcare services are provided by rendering them more readily available, user-friendly, and productive. In this article, we will discuss the impact that telemedicine has had on the healthcare business, as well as its advantages, disadvantages, and the potential for further development in the field of healthcare provision.

1. **Getting Familiar with Telemedicine**
   The delivery of medical care over long distances using telecommunications technology, most frequently through the use of video conferencing and other forms of digital communication equipment is known as telemedicine. It eliminates or significantly reduces the need for healthcare personnel to physically examine, diagnose, and treat patients, allowing them to do it from a distance.
2. **The Advantages of Using Telemedicine**
   2.1. Increased Availability of Medical Care
   The elimination of geographical obstacles through telemedicine makes it possible for those living in underserved or distant places to have access to medical care. This is especially useful in more remote areas of the country where there are fewer medical services.
   2.2. The Ease of Use and the Adaptability
   Patients are able to book virtual appointments whenever it is most convenient for them, which eliminates the requirement for costly and time-consuming travel. The patients' work and family commitments can be easily accommodated with the flexible hours that are offered through telemedicine.
   2.3. Effective Distribution of Available Resources
   By decreasing the number of non-emergency in-person visits, medical facilities like hospitals and clinics can better allocate their available resources. Because of this, healthcare facilities are freed up to concentrate on treating essential patients

and responding to emergencies.

2.4. Decreased Expenses

Patients and healthcare systems alike benefit from the financial strain being alleviated by telemedicine. Patients don't have to pay the costs of traveling, and medical professionals can give their services at a lower overall cost.

2.5. Maintaining Consistency in Care

Patients suffering from chronic illnesses might benefit from constant monitoring made possible by telemedicine, which also encourages timely intervention and lowers the risk of consequences.

2.6. Increased Participation from Patients

Patients frequently feel more at ease sharing their health concerns over the phone, which ultimately leads to more open and honest talks with the healthcare providers they are working with.

3. **Repercussions for the Provision of Healthcare**

3.1 The Difference Between Primary Care and Urgent Care

Primary care and urgent care have both benefited from the expansion of services offered through telemedicine. Patients don't even have to leave the comfort of their own homes to get treatment, guidance, or refills on their prescriptions for common conditions.

3.2. Consultations Concerning Specialized Matters

Even if they are located in a remote location, medical specialists and other experts in a variety of sectors are now accessible thanks to telemedicine. Patients get access to the most qualified experts in their disciplines for consultations and suggestions regarding treatment options.

3.3. Services Relating to Mental Health

The sector of mental health is one that has benefited tremendously from the application of telemedicine. Counseling and therapy sessions can now be conducted remotely, making them more accessible to people in need.

3.4 Management of Chronic Diseases

Patients who have chronic diseases, such diabetes or hypertension, can use telemedicine to more closely monitor their health and obtain timely intervention, thereby minimizing the likelihood that they will experience complications.

3.5. Protective Medical Measures

Patients are able to more easily access preventative care because to the convenience provided by telemedicine, which makes it possible for them to have frequent checkups and screenings.

3.6 Care After Surgery and After Patients Have Recuperated

Patients who have undergone surgery may benefit from post-operative treatment and follow-up appointments that are conducted remotely, as this eliminates the necessity for in-person visits and the discomfort that comes along with them.

4. **Obstacles and Causes for Concern**

Despite the many advantages it offers, telemedicine is not without its share of obstacles and worries, all of which need to be addressed.

4.1. Obstacles Caused by Technology

It's important to note that not all patients have access to the high-speed internet connections and essential technologies for productive telemedicine sessions. Access to medical care may become unequal as a result of this.

4.2. Safety and Personal Confidentiality

It is of the utmost importance to guard the confidentiality of patients' medical records and prevent their information from falling into the wrong hands. To ensure the safety of private patient information, healthcare providers need to put in place stringent security protocols.

4.3. Authorization and Administration of Regulation

The practice of telemedicine frequently spans the boundaries of states or countries, which might make it more difficult to comply with licensing and regulatory requirements. In order to ensure that they are acting ethically and legally, healthcare providers are required to traverse difficult legal frameworks.

4.4. The Boundaries of the Diagnostic Process

Telemedicine may be able to manage many parts of the delivery of medical treatment; but, it has its limits when it comes to identifying some disorders, particularly those that need for physical examinations or laboratory tests.

4.5. There is Little to No Physical Contact

Some people believe that the interpersonal connection that may be built between patients and healthcare providers during in-person visits is impossible to achieve when using telemedicine.

5. **The Prospects for the Field of Telemedicine**

5.1 Integration of Artificial Intelligence and Machine Learning

The applications of artificial intelligence (AI) and machine learning will become increasingly significant in the field of telemedicine. These technologies will help in the diagnosis and treatment of patients, as well as in the prediction of health outcomes and the automation of administrative activities.

5.2 Wearable technology and remote monitoring come in at number

The spread of wearable gadgets and remote monitoring technology will offer medical professionals with real-time data on the health of patients, enabling them to provide care that is both more proactive and more individualized.

5.3 Virtual Reality (VR) and Augmented Reality (AR) are both types of mixed reality.

Both virtual reality and augmented reality have potential uses in telemedicine, including improved diagnoses, improved medical education, and improved assistance for remote surgical procedures. The distance between in-person and remote medical care will be further narrowed by these technological advancements.

5.4. Increased Capabilities Within Specialty Categories

There will be an increase in the number of medical disciplines that use telemedicine, such as radiology, pathology, and anesthesia. Because of this, the benefits of remote healthcare will be extended to a wider variety of medical specialties.

5.5. The Development of Policies and Regulations

The policies and regulations that govern telemedicine will continue to develop in order to keep up with the rapid rate at which technology is progressing. This covers regulations concerning reimbursement, confidentiality, and licensure.

5.6. The Application of Telemedicine in Developing Countries

By providing access to healthcare services and knowledge that were previously unavailable, telemedicine will assist in filling the existing gaps in healthcare delivery that exist in underdeveloped countries.

The delivery of healthcare services has been revolutionized by the advent of telemedicine, which has made these services more easily accessible, comfortable, and effective. Access to healthcare has been enhanced, expenditures have been cut, and patient participation has been boosted as a result.

The widespread implementation of telemedicine has had an effect on primary care, specialty consultations, mental health services, and the management of chronic diseases. There are problems with regards to access to technology, security, and regulations, but these are being fixed as the industry continues to advance in its development.

The future of telemedicine appears to be bright, with artificial intelligence (AI) and machine learning, virtual reality (VR), augmented reality (AR), wearable technologies, and increased specialist services all poised to play crucial roles. The continuous development of new policies and regulations will provide additional backing for the incorporation of telemedicine into the existing healthcare system. Telemedicine will continue to revolutionize the method in which healthcare services are offered and accessed, bringing about radical changes to the healthcare business and enhancing the quality of treatment for patients all over the world as technology continues to advance.

5.2 Smart Cities and Infrastructure

The idea of "smart cities" has developed as a potentially game-changing approach to solve the multifaceted difficulties of urban living in light of the rapid urbanization that is occurring all over the world. The use of technology and data in smart cities helps to improve the overall quality of life, as well as infrastructure and efforts toward promoting sustainability. In this piece, we will discuss the idea of smart cities, as well as their influence on existing infrastructure and the part they play in determining the trajectory of urban life in the future.

1. **An Explanation of What Smart Cities Are**
   Smart cities are urban regions that make use of technology, data, and connection to improve the quality of life for their citizens, better the operations of the city, and create an environment that is more sustainable and efficient. These cities use a variety of digital technologies, such as devices connected to the Internet of Things (IoT), sensors, data analytics, and networking infrastructure, to improve the efficiency of their urban planning, resources, and service delivery.
2. **Repercussions for the Infrastructure**
   2.1. Mobility and Modes of Transportation
   The incorporation of technology into urban transportation networks is a key component of the smart city concept, which aims to increase general mobility while simultaneously alleviating traffic congestion. This involves the implementation of intelligent traffic management, the monitoring of public transit in real time, and the promotion of environmentally friendly modes of transportation such as electric vehicles and bike-sharing programs.
   2.2. Power Sources and Providers
   In order to lower their overall energy consumption and have a less negative impact on the surrounding environment, "smart cities" use energy-efficient technologies such as smart grids and renewable energy sources. They also use data to monitor and optimize water supply, waste management, and utility operations, which helps them conserve resources and cut costs.
   2.3. Connectivity and Information Technology Infrastructure
   Smart cities rely heavily on their robust digital infrastructure as their primary support system. Real-time data is made available for the management of city operations, the improvement of public services, and the overall enhancement of the urban experience by means of high-speed internet access, 5G networks, and a huge array of sensors and Internet of Things devices.
   2.4. Educational Opportunities and Medical Care
   The incorporation of technology into smart cities is aimed at enhancing the quality of medical treatment and educational opportunities. The use of telemedicine, digital health records, and online learning platforms all contribute to an increase in the availability of high-quality medical care and educational opportunities. This not only improves the overall quality of life but also makes a contribution to the expansion of the economy.
   2.5 Safety and Protection of the General Public
   The public's safety can be improved with the use of data analytics and surveillance technology in smart cities. This includes predictive policing, improved catastrophe management, and emergency response optimization, among other things.
   2.6. Planning for a Sustainable Urban Future
   Sustainable urban planning techniques are adopted by smart cities. These

plans highlight the inclusion of green spaces, walkability, and environmentally friendly building practices. This leads to a decrease in urban sprawl, an increase in available green space, and an overall improvement in the livability of the urban environment.

2.7. Participation of the Citizens

The incorporation of city residents into decision-making processes and the promotion of community involvement can both be facilitated through the use of digital platforms in smart cities. Because of this transparency and accessibility, residents have a greater feeling of ownership in their town, which also helps to develop a deeper sense of community.

3. **The Advantages of Living in a Smart City**

The development of smart cities results in a wide range of advantages, which accrue not only to inhabitants but also to municipal governments.

3.1. An Increased Satisfaction with Life

Residents in smart cities enjoy an improved quality of life as a result of the reduction of traffic congestion, the improvement of public services, and the creation of an urban environment that is more sustainable and friendly to the environment.

3.2. The Long-Term Viability of the Environment

Cleaner air, higher water quality, and an overall healthier environment are the results of smart cities' implementation of environmentally friendly technologies and sustainable business practices, which lower their environmental imprint.

3.3. Effective Administration of Available Resources

The management of resources in smart cities is optimized, which results in decreased consumption of electricity and water, decreased operational expenses, and more effective use of public monies.

3.4. The Development of the Economy

Smart cities, which are driven by technology-based initiatives, are able to offer job possibilities, encourage entrepreneurial activity, and attract creative enterprises, all of which contribute to economic growth.

3.5. Protective Measures and Safeguards

Surveillance, predictive policing, and improved emergency response systems are some of the ways in which smart cities contribute to increased public safety and security.

4. **Obstacles and Things to Take Into Account**

Even though the idea of smart cities holds a lot of potential, it must first overcome a number of obstacles and take into account a number of factors.

4.1. Investments in the Infrastructure

Investing a large amount of capital is required in order to construct and improve the appropriate digital and physical infrastructure. In many cities, the implementation of these improvements is hampered by financial constraints.

4.2. Protection of Personal Information and Data

Concerns over individuals' right to privacy and the safety of their data have been raised as a result of the collection of enormous volumes of data for use in smart city operations. It is of the utmost importance to safeguard the personal information of residents and make responsible use of it.

4.3 Inclusion in the Digital Age

Residents may not all have the same level of access to technology or the same level of digital literacy, which are both necessary for full participation in smart city programs. It is necessary to ensure digital inclusion in order to prevent existing inequities from becoming even more pronounced.

4.4. Standardization and Interoperability

When multiple technologies and platforms are incorporated into the framework of a smart city, there is the potential for interoperability problems to occur. The establishment of standards and protocols for open data is an essential step toward achieving seamless integration.

5. The Path Forward for Intelligent Cities

5.1. Robotics and other Forms of Artificial Intelligence

Autonomous vehicles, predictive maintenance, and sophisticated decision-making systems are

just a few examples of the ways in which artificial intelligence (AI) and automation will play an increasingly important role in the development of smart cities.

5.2. Distributed Power Sources and Localized Power Grids

Decentralized energy systems and microgrids, which boost energy resilience and minimize dependency on centralized power sources, will become the norm in smart cities as they make the transition to being really smart.

5.3. The Economy Based on Circularity

The implementation of the concepts of a circular economy will encourage the reduction, reuse, and recycling of resources, hence reducing waste and the negative impact on the environment.

5.4 Municipalities With Greater Inclusivity and Equity

The future of smart cities will center on making certain that technology and innovation are applied in such a way as to produce urban settings that are more welcoming and equal for all of the city's people.

The development of smart cities is laying the way for a future that is both environmentally friendly and technologically advanced. They do this by utilizing data and technological advancements to better infrastructure, transportation, energy, healthcare, and other public services. Smart cities continue to develop and innovate even if they confront obstacles in the areas of investment, privacy, and digital inclusion.

There is no doubt that the future of smart cities will bring about additional breakthroughs in artificial intelligence, decentralized energy systems, concepts of circular economies, and a deeper emphasis on inclusivity and equity. As the rate of urbanization continues to climb, the process of transforming cities into environments that are smarter, more sustainable, and technologically advanced is an essential step towards improving the quality of life for all citizens and creating a more promising future.

5.3 Manufacturing and Industry 4.0

The manufacturing sector is going through a period of deep change as a result of the introduction of the idea known as Industry 4.0. This is a concept that makes use of cutting-edge technologies to develop intelligent and connected factories. This revolution in manufacturing is characterized by the use of artificial intelligence (AI), automation, data analytics, the Internet of Things (IoT), and other technologies in order to improve productivity, efficiency, and quality. In this piece, we will investigate the effects that Industry 4.0 has had on the manufacturing industry as well as the key factors that are driving this transition.

1. **What exactly is meant by "Industry 4.0"?**
   The term "Industry 4.0," which is also commonly known as "the Fourth Industrial Revolution," refers to a significant change in the way that industrial processes are conceived of and carried out. It does this by utilizing digital technology and data-driven insights to improve each and every part of the manufacturing process, from the design and production of products to the management of supply chains and customer service.
2. **Principal Components of the Fourth Industrial Revolution**
   2.1. IoT stands for the Internet of Things
   The Internet of Things (IoT) involves connecting commonplace machines and things to the internet in order to give them the ability to collect and share data. In the manufacturing industry, Internet of Things devices can be used to track inventory, check the health of equipment, and improve supply chain logistics.
   2.2. Analyses of the Data
   The manufacturing process generates a tremendous amount of data, which must be collected and analyzed before data analytics can be performed. Using this data, patterns may be identified, procedures can be optimized, and decisions can be made with more knowledge.
   2.3 Artificial Intelligence (AI)
   AI technologies, such as machine learning, make it possible for machines and systems to teach themselves from data, adjust to new circumstances, and come to their own choices. Artificial intelligence has the potential to improve predictive maintenance, quality control, and demand forecasting in the manufacturing industry.
   2.4. Robotics and Automated Processes
   Industry 4.0 places a significant emphasis on the use of robotics and automation. Automated systems are able to conduct repetitive jobs with a high degree

of accuracy, whereas robotics are able to handle complicated procedures, which leads to enhanced efficiency and consistency.

2.5. Augmented Reality (AR) and Virtual Reality (VR)

Training, maintenance, and remote collaboration are some of the applications for augmented and virtual reality technologies. AR glasses give employees access to real-time data and instructions, which in turn helps to cut down on errors and boost overall efficiency.

3. **Effect on Industrial Production**

3.1. An Increase in Productivity

Automation and data-driven processes save the amount of time needed for manufacturing, reduce the number of errors made, and improve overall efficiency. The production schedules of smart factories are able to be adjusted in real time to accommodate varying levels of customer demand.

3.2. Enhancements Made to the Quality Control

Real-time quality monitoring is made possible with the combination of Internet of Things sensors and artificial intelligence. Instantaneous detection and correction of flaws leads to a reduction in product waste and an improvement in product quality.

3.3. The Practice of Predictive Maintenance

The ability of connected equipment to anticipate when they will require servicing helps eliminate unanticipated malfunctions and minimizes the amount of time spent offline. This preventative strategy cuts down on the number of production interruptions.

3.4. Improved Capability for Individualization

The Fourth Industrial Revolution makes it easier to produce highly individualized goods. Modern production methods are able to be adapted to the specific requirements of each unique customer, which results in higher levels of customer satisfaction.

3.5. Optimization of the Supply Chain

The utilization of data analytics and communication in real time enables improved supply chain management. The ability to quickly adapt to shifting market conditions and lower inventory costs is available to manufacturers.

3.6. Manufacturing That Is Sustainable

The usage of resources, the consumption of energy, and the amount of trash produced may all be optimized in smart factories, contributing to a manufacturing process that is more sustainable.

4. **Obstacles and Things to Take Into Account**

While Industry 4.0 does present a number of significant advantages, there are also a number of problems and factors to take into consideration.

4.1. The Primary Financial Investment

The shift to Industry 4.0 calls for substantial initial investments in terms of both technology and training, in addition to physical infrastructure. For businesses to successfully navigate this change, strategic planning and resource allocation is required.

4.2. Security in Cyberspace

As factories grow more connected to one another, they open themselves up to the possibility of being attacked digitally. The protection of sensitive data and the upkeep of operational integrity both need the implementation of stringent cybersecurity measures.

4.3. Skills Needed in the Workplace

It is necessary to have a qualified workforce that is able to operate and maintain modern systems in order to implement the technologies of Industry 4.0. Companies have a responsibility to make financial investments in the education and training of their staff.

4.4. Data Privacy and Security

Concerns around data privacy and ownership are raised as a result of the collection and utilization of massive volumes of data in smart factories. In order to effectively handle these problems, manufacturers need to create specific policies and procedures.

5. **The Prospects for the 4.0 Version of Industry**

Continued technological advancement and market penetration will characterize the future of Industry 4.0.

5.1. Implementation of New and Evolving Technologies

The capabilities of smart factories will continue to improve as a result of Industry 4.0's further integration of developing technologies such as 5G connection, blockchain, and edge computing.

5.2. An Increased Capacity for Sustainability

The consumption of energy will be cut even more, trash will be kept to a minimum, and ecologically responsible procedures will be put into place in smart factories.

5.3. Enhanced Human-Machine Collaboration

In the future, there will be more collaboration between humans and machines, with AI and robots complementing human capabilities in production processes. This will occur in the future.

5.4. Resilience of the Supply Chain

Building supply chains that are resilient and flexible, able to endure shocks and uncertainties, will be given a significant amount of focus as part of the Industry 4.0 initiative.

The fourth industrial revolution, also known as Industry 4.0, is revolutionizing the manufacturing industry by providing better efficiency, improved quality control, expanded customization, and predictive maintenance. Despite the fact that there will be obstacles to overcome, manufacturers will be able to capitalize on the benefits of this revolutionary revolution if they plan well, invest in technology, and train their employees. Manufacturing is expected to have a future that is greener, more efficient, and better connected to the digital world because to the ongoing development and expansion of Industry 4.0.

5.4 Entertainment and Media

The upheaval brought on by the rise of digital technology has had a significant impact on the entertainment and media scene in recent years, causing it to undergo a remarkable shift. The traditional forms of media such as print, television, and radio have been supplemented and, in some cases, superseded by their digital analogues. This transformation has ushered in a new era, which is characterized by accessibility, interaction, and the consumption of content that is tailored to the individual.

The widespread availability of digital platforms and streaming services has made it possible to access a vast library of content at any time and from virtually any location. We now have easy access to a wide variety of entertainment options, including music, movies, television shows, and news, which enables a more individualized and on-demand experience.

The ways in which we take in news and interact with material have been profoundly impacted by the rise of social media. Not only has it made the distribution of information more accessible to the general public, but it has also opened up new doors for content creators, influencers, and user-generated material.

The rise of eSports and the proliferation of mobile gaming have been major contributors to the gaming industry's meteoric expansion in recent years. The technologies of virtual reality (VR) and augmented reality (AR) are pushing the boundaries of what can be considered an immersive entertainment experience.

Despite the fact that these technological breakthroughs have widened access to entertainment and media, they also create a number of concerns, including problems concerning data privacy, the moderation of content, and the propagation of disinformation. In order for the industry to maintain its vitality, diversity, and ethical standards amidst the ongoing transformation of the digital landscape, it must continue to adapt and innovate.

5.5 Agriculture and Environmental Monitoring

The agricultural industry is increasingly relying on cutting-edge technology in order to enhance both its productivity and its compatibility with the natural environment. Monitoring the environment in particular has developed into an essential component of contemporary agricultural practices. It entails evaluating, analyzing, and managing the environmental elements of farming activities through the utilization of a variety of instruments and approaches. In this section, we will discuss the vital function that environmental monitoring plays in agriculture and how it contributes to the development of a more sustainable future.

1. **Agriculture with Great Accuracy**
   Monitoring the surrounding environment is essential to the practice of precision agriculture, which strives to improve agricultural methods for maximum productivity with minimal adverse effects on the surrounding ecosystem. This strategy compiles information regarding the state of the soil, the weather patterns, and the overall health of the crop by utilizing various technological tools such as satellite photography, drones, and sensors. Farmers can now make educated decisions about irrigation, fertilizer, and pest control using this data, which will result in less wasted resources and less negative effects on the environment.
2. **The Administration of Water**
   Water is a crucial resource for agricultural production, and efficient management of this resource is necessary to ensure the long-term health of the ecosystem. Monitoring instruments assist farmers in determining the amount of moisture in the soil, estimating the amount of water that will be required for irrigation, and reducing the amount of water that is wasted. Agricultural practices can be brought into alignment with responsible water usage and, as a result, less strain can be placed on water resources. This can be accomplished through the application of data-driven insights.
3. **Methods for the Preventive and Curative Treatment of Illness**
   Monitoring of the environment helps in the early detection and treatment of illnesses and pests that can affect crops. Farmers are able to notice abnormalities and respond appropriately in a timely manner to prevent the further spread of pests by utilizing sensors and remote monitoring systems. This preventative strategy lessens the need for chemical treatments, which is beneficial not only to the environment but also to the crop yields.
4. **Preservation of the Soil and Its Health**
   Monitoring the health of the soil is an essential component of sustainable agriculture. Environmental sensors and data analysis provide information about the levels of soil nutrients, the risks of soil erosion, and the degradation of soil. Farmers are able to ensure that the soil will remain healthy for future generations if they implement procedures such as soil conservation and precise fertilization methods.
5. **The Administration of Ecosystems and Biodiversity**
   Agriculture and the surrounding natural environment are deeply intertwined. Monitoring the environment provides farmers with the tools they need to conserve local biodiversity by managing their property in a way that is beneficial to ecosystems. Agriculture and environment are able to live in peace with one another if farmers cut back on the use of poisonous pesticides and create areas that are welcoming to animals.
6. **Actions to Reduce the Impacts of Climate Change**
   Agriculture is one of the industries that is impacted as well as one that

contributes to climate change. Monitoring the environment gives farmers the ability to adjust to the ever-changing weather conditions and cut their emissions of greenhouse gases. Additionally, it makes it possible to make efforts toward carbon sequestration through measures such as reforestation and conservation tillage.

7. **Obstacles to Overcome and Potential Future Developments**

Environmental monitoring in agriculture has a number of advantages, but it also has a number of disadvantages, such as the high cost of adopting new technology, the difficulty of managing data, and the requirement for ongoing education. Nevertheless, these problems are gradually being overcome as a result of developments in technology that are making it more accessible. Integrating even more cutting-edge technology, such as artificial intelligence (AI), machine learning, and blockchain, into agriculture will allow for improved data analysis, more accurate predictive modeling, and more open supply chains. This is the future of agriculture.

Monitoring the environment is having a transformative effect on the agricultural industry by increasing productivity, decreasing adverse effects on the environment, and fostering sustainability. Farmers are better positioned to make informed decisions that strike a balance between their economic interests and environmental stewardship as a result of their embrace of cutting-edge technologies and practices that are data-driven. As the world's population continues to climb, the significance of ecologically responsible agriculture will continue to increase. As a result, environmental monitoring will become an essential instrument in the process of sculpting a future that is sustainable.

Chapter 6

Security and Privacy in the 5G and Cloud Era

The advent of 5G and cloud computing has ushered in a new paradigm of connectivity and data management, delivering speeds, capacities, and accessibility that have never been seen before. Nevertheless, this digital transition comes with intrinsic problems to security and privacy that call for comprehensive solutions. As individuals and companies navigate this terrain, protecting sensitive data and maintaining privacy have become essential imperatives that must be met. In this extensive investigation, we delve into the numerous dimensions of security and privacy in the context of the transformation brought about by 5G and the cloud. We investigate the difficulties, solutions, and best practices that may be utilized to assure trust and protection in a world that is increasingly interconnected.

1. **A Contextual Overview of 5G and the Cloud Landscape**
   The combination of 5G and cloud technologies has fundamentally altered the nature of the digital landscape. As a result, individuals and companies now have access to a level of connection, data processing capacity, and service availability that has never been seen before. This transition has made new opportunities for innovation and growth available, but it has also made data and systems more susceptible to attack, making it necessary to take stringent precautions to protect users' privacy and safety.
2. **Having an understanding of the implications for security**
   In this day and age of 5G and the cloud, the proliferation of connected devices, the exponential rise of data, and the interconnectedness of systems have dramatically increased the attack surface for potential security breaches. Data breaches, virus attacks, and unauthorized access are three examples of the types of threats that pose significant dangers to both persons and enterprises.
3. **Challenges to Privacy in an Ever-Increasingly Connected World**
   Concerns have been expressed over the privacy of data and the ethical use of

personal information as a result of the hyperconnected world made possible by 5G and cloud technologies. Discussions concerning user permission, data ownership, and the requirement for rigorous privacy legislation have been generated as a direct result of the collecting, storage, and analysis of enormous amounts of data.

4. **The Importance of Secure Data Transmission and Encryption**
   In this day and age of 5G and the cloud, encryption serves as an essential safety measure, ensuring that data is protected both while it is in transit and while it is stored. End-to-end encryption, data masking, and tokenization are critical data security techniques that should be used wherever possible to maintain data integrity and prevent unwanted access to sensitive information.
5. **Putting in place a Multi-Factor Authentication System**
   The use of multi-factor authentication, also known as MFA, has become increasingly popular as a reliable safeguard against identity theft and unlawful access. Organizations have the ability to strengthen their security protocols by using multi-factor authentication (MFA), which requires various forms of verification before granting access to critical data and systems.
6. **Intelligence on potential dangers and proactive surveillance**
   Both threat intelligence and proactive monitoring are extremely important components in the process of locating and neutralizing potential security risks in real time. Organizations are able to quickly respond to potential security breaches and protect important data from being accessed by malicious actors when they make use of sophisticated monitoring tools and threat detection systems.
7. **Developing an Infrastructure Capable of Withstanding Cyberattacks**
   It is absolutely necessary for businesses to have a dependable cybersecurity infrastructure in order to function effectively in the 5G and cloud environments. In order to enhance defenses against cyberattacks and weaknesses, it is necessary to construct reliable firewalls, install intrusion detection systems, and perform routine security audits.
8. **The Importance of Being in Compliance with Regulations**
   In this day and age of 5G and the cloud, it is very necessary for businesses that deal with sensitive data to strictly adhere to the regulatory compliance standards that have been established, such as the General Data Protection Regulation (GDPR) and the California Consumer Privacy Act (CCPA). Compliance guarantees that data is treated in accordance with the law, in an open and honest manner, and with the utmost respect for the individual's right to privacy.
9. **Providing Instruction and Training for Staff**
   When it comes to cultivating a culture that is security conscious within enterprises, education and training of staff on the most recent security protocols and privacy best practices is of the utmost importance. Employees can be given the ability to spot possible security threats, adhere to privacy guidelines, and

respond effectively to security incidents through the implementation of comprehensive training programs.

10. **Addressing Concerns Regarding Ethical Behavior**
    Ethical concerns over data usage, AI-driven analytics, and user profiling have emerged as significant issues in the era of 5G and cloud computing. Ethical data practices need to be prioritized by organizations in order to guarantee that data is handled in a responsible and transparent manner and that artificial intelligence algorithms are free of biases and discriminatory patterns.
11. **Collaborative Work and the Exchange of Information**
    The industry as a whole must work together and share information in order to effectively counteract the ever-evolving dangers to information security. Organizations are able to cooperatively develop their security postures and remain one step ahead of sophisticated cyber attacks if they share insights, best practices, and threat intelligence with one another.
12. **The State of Cybersecurity and Personal Privacy in the Age of 5G and the Cloud**

The future of security and privacy in the era of 5G and the cloud will witness the integration of powerful AI-driven security solutions, blockchain-based data management, and quantum encryption techniques. This will occur as a result of the continual evolution of technology. Because of these improvements, the protection of sensitive data will be strengthened, it will be possible to conduct secure decentralized transactions, and privacy standards will reach new heights.

To cultivate trust and confidence in digital interactions in this age of 5G and the cloud, it is essential to implement stringent security measures and to protect individuals' privacy. Organizations are able to successfully negotiate the intricacies of today's hyperconnected world with resilience and integrity if they put in place all-encompassing security measures, place a high priority on data protection, and adhere to ethical data practices. When it comes to ensuring the safety of essential data assets and laying a solid groundwork for the development of future digital connectivity, a proactive and flexible approach to data security and privacy will be absolutely necessary as technological development proceeds unabated.

6.1 Challenges in Securing 5G and Cloud Networks

Connectivity and data management have both been significantly improved as a result of revolutionary new developments brought about by the convergence of 5G and cloud technologies. These technological advancements hold the promise of great opportunities for individuals, corporations, and governments alike; nevertheless, they also present a wide range of security challenges. Securing 5G and cloud networks is a complicated and diverse activity that requires a full awareness of the potential dangers and a proactive approach to mitigating them. This is necessary in order to achieve success. In this in-depth investigation, we look into the primary issues and worries related with protecting 5G and cloud networks. We also investigate the complicated terrain of dangers and the strategies that can be used to protect this hyperconnected world.

1. **An Increased Number of Points of Attack**
   The greatly increased attack surface is one of the key obstacles that must be overcome in order to ensure the security of 5G and cloud networks. The interconnection of devices, systems, and data across a 5G and cloud infrastructure increases the number of potential entry points that might be exploited by attackers. Attackers can take advantage of weaknesses in every network element, from Internet of Things devices to cloud servers, which puts the entire ecosystem at risk of being compromised.
2. **Weaknesses in Internet of Things**
   The explosion in the number of Internet of Things (IoT) devices has given rise to a wide variety of new privacy and safety concerns. Because of their limited computing power and lack of other security mechanisms, many of these devices are susceptible to being exploited. Devices connected to the internet of things that lack adequate security measures leave the network vulnerable to serious threats because they can allow hostile users to obtain access to the system.
3. **Compliance and Protection of Personal Information**
   Concerns about data privacy and compliance with legal standards, such as those outlined in the General Data Protection Regulation (GDPR) and the California Consumer Privacy Act (CCPA), have been raised as a result of the gathering, storage, and processing of enormous amounts of data in cloud networks. When firms fail to comply with regulations, they risk suffering hefty financial fines as well as damage to their reputations.
4. **Dangers Coming From Within**
   Threats posed by insiders continue to be a key obstacle in the process of protecting cloud and 5G networks. It is possible for employees or authorized users to cause data breaches and system compromises through malicious or careless activities on their end.
   In order to protect against insider threats, organizations need to strike a balance between trusting employees and verifying their claims.
5. **More Advanced Forms of Online Attacks**
   A new wave of highly sophisticated cyberattacks has emerged in this new era of 5G and cloud computing. Threats such as advanced persistent threats (APTs), ransomware, and zero-day vulnerabilities pose significant challenges to the integrity of computer networks. The strategies that attackers use to circumvent traditional security measures are continually being refined and improved.
6. **Protection of the Supply Chain**
   A increasing challenge is ensuring the security of the supply chain, which includes everything from the hardware components to the software vendors.

Because compromised portions of the supply chain can introduce vulnerabilities into network infrastructure, it is absolutely necessary to implement supply chain processes that are both visible and secure.

7. **Problems with the Cloud's Configuration**
   Cloud settings that have been improperly configured are a common cause of security flaws. Accidental disclosure of data can occur as a result of human mistake; therefore, cloud providers and users need to collaborate to ensure that configurations are optimized for security.
8. **The Limited Availability of Resources and Their Scalability**
   Scalability issues and a lack of available resources might be obstacles in the process of safeguarding cloud networks. Cloud service providers have the responsibility of striking a balance between the availability of resources and the implementation of security measures, making certain that the rapid scaling of resources does not jeopardize security procedures.
9. **The Complicated Nature of Regulations**
   When it comes to the protection of 5G and cloud networks, one of the most difficult challenges is navigating the convoluted web of international and sector-specific rules. It is imperative for organizations to remain current on the ever-shifting compliance standards and modify their security protocols accordingly.
10. **Identity and Access Management That Is Complicated**
    It can be challenging to manage user identities and access privileges across a complicated network ecosystem. In order to successfully safeguard resources while still allowing users to access them in accordance with their authorization, identity and access management (IAM) systems need to be both resilient and adaptable.
11. **Encryption and the Protection of Personal Data**
    Despite the fact that encryption is one of the most important components of data security, ensuring that it is correctly implemented across 5G and cloud networks can be difficult. Keeping encryption methods resilient, safeguarding data while it is in transit and while it is at rest, and managing encryption keys are all extremely important considerations.
12. **The Challenge Posed by Preexisting Computer Systems**
    A large number of companies are still dependent on older systems and technologies, despite the fact that these do not have the security features necessary for modern cloud and 5G settings. It is a difficult job to ensure the safety of these legacy systems while still preserving connectivity with more recent technology.
13. **New Dangers Posed by Artificial Intelligence and Quantum Computing**
    Both the advancement of artificial intelligence (AI) and quantum computing bring with them new security possibilities as well as new potential dangers. Artificial intelligence can be used to improve security measures, but it can also be utilized by attackers to their advantage. It is possible that present encryption

systems could be broken using quantum computing; therefore, it is necessary to design encryption that is resistant to quantum computing.

14. **Recommended Procedures and Risk Avoidance Techniques**
    Conducting frequent Risk Assessments It is important to perform comprehensive risk assessments on a frequent basis in order to discover weaknesses and prioritize security measures.
    Network Segmentation It is important to implement network segmentation in order to restrict the ability of attackers to move laterally within the network.
    Training and Awareness for Users It is important to train and inform users about the best security practices and the significance of maintaining good cybersecurity hygiene.
    Adopt a security model known as zero trust, which checks and authenticates all users and devices irrespective of their physical location. This is the recommended course of action.
    Instead of considering security as an afterthought, implement it from the beginning of the design process for 5G and cloud networks using the "security by design" methodology.
    Regular Patch Management entails ensuring that all software and systems are kept up to date with the latest security patches to address any vulnerabilities that may have been discovered.
    Plan for Responding to Incidents You should draft and practice a plan for responding to incidents in order to ensure a prompt and effective response to any breaches in security.
    Sharing of Threat Intelligence and Collaborative Efforts: To keep one step ahead of ever-evolving cyber threats, it is important to collaborate with peers in your sector and share threat intelligence.
    Regulatory Compliance In order to prevent legal repercussions, it is critical to maintain compliance with data protection legislation and industry standards.
15. **The Prospects for Safer 5G and Cloud Networks in the Future**

In order to ensure the continued safety of 5G and cloud networks in the future, ongoing innovation and adaptability to new dangers will be required. Learning by machine and artificial intelligence will play a crucial part in the process of discovering and mitigating real-time security vulnerabilities. It will be increasingly vital to use blockchain technology for the purpose of secure data management and encryption that is resistant to quantum computing.

6.2 Strategies for Ensuring Data Privacy

Maintaining data privacy has emerged as an issue of utmost importance for individuals, corporations, and governments in this day and age, when personal information has developed into a valuable commodity and data breaches have become an alarmingly frequent occurrence. The security of personal information is more important than it has ever been as a result of the rising digitization of our lives, which includes everything from online shopping to interactions on social media. This article digs deep into the methods that can be used to protect the privacy of one's data. It examines both individual and organizational ways to protecting sensitive data and preserving one's privacy in a world that is becoming increasingly linked.

1. **The Foundations of Data Privacy**
   It is necessary to have a fundamental understanding of what data privacy implies before delving into specific tactics. The protection of sensitive information, whether it belongs to an individual or an organization, against illegal access, use, disclosure, or alteration is what is meant by the term "data privacy." Personal information such as names, addresses, and other financial details, as well as intellectual property, trade secrets, and other types of information, can be included in this category of data.
2. **Individual Methods for Protecting the Privacy of Data**
   Strong Passwords It is imperative that each of your online accounts use a robust and one-of-a-kind password. You can use a password manager to help you generate and securely store passwords that are difficult.
   Two-Factor Authentication (also known as 2FA): Whenever it is an option, turn on 2FA to offer an additional layer of protection to your online accounts.
   Maintaining an Up-to-Date Software System It is important to maintain an operating system and software that are both up to date in order to patch any security vulnerabilities.
   Awareness: When it comes to the information you provide online, exercise extreme caution. It is best to refrain from discussing private matters in open forums and on social media.
   Privacy when Browsing: To reduce the amount of information that can be tracked while you browse the web, utilize web browsers, search engines, and browser extensions that prioritize privacy.
   Wi-Fi Security: Protect the wireless network in your home by using a robust password and encrypting the data. When conducting important business, you should avoid using public Wi-Fi.
   Encrypting Your Emails To keep the information included in your emails secure, you should encrypt them using a service or a tool.
   Read the Privacy rules: Make sure you are aware of the privacy rules that are associated with the services and websites that you use so that you are aware of how your data is being used and shared.
   Data Backups: Make sure that you back up your data on a regular basis to defend against the possibility of losing data as a result of security breaches or accidents.

Documents Should Be Shredded To safely dispose of physical documents that contain sensitive information, you should shred the documents first.

3. **Organizational Methods to Protect Confidential Information**

   Privacy by Design is an approach that encourages businesses to include data privacy concerns into the early stages of the product and service development process.

   Classification of Data: Data should be classified according to how sensitive it is and how important it is. This assists in determining the order of priority for preventative measures.

   Access Control: Make sure that only authorized workers are able to access sensitive data by implementing stringent access controls and limiting who can access it.

   Encryption of Data: Encrypt data both while it is at rest and while it is in transit to prevent unwanted access to it both within the organization and while it is being transmitted outside of it.

   Conducting Regular Audits and Assessments: It is important to conduct regular audits and assessments of data privacy and security in order to uncover potential vulnerabilities and compliance issues.

   Establishing Clear and Transparent Privacy rules It is important to establish clear and transparent privacy rules that explain how data gathered from customers is handled and protected.

   Data Minimization entails collecting and storing only the minimum amount of data required to accomplish the goals of your organization. Delete any information that is no longer necessary.

   Plan for Responding to Incidents Create a plan for responding to data breaches and other violations of privacy in a timely and efficient manner by creating an incident response plan.

   Training for staff: Educate staff about the best practices for maintaining data privacy as well as the organization's data protection rules.

   Management of suppliers: Make sure that any third-party suppliers or partners comply with your data privacy requirements and conduct frequent audits of their compliance.

   Compliance with rules Ensure that you are in compliance with any data protection rules and privacy legislation that are applicable to your business sector and location, such as GDPR, CCPA, HIPAA, and others.

4. **Technologies for Protecting Private Information**

   Virtual Private Networks (VPNs) encrypt your internet connection, making it more difficult for third parties to keep track of what you do online.

   End-to-End Encryption: Messaging apps such as Signal and WhatsApp offer end-to-end encryption for users who are concerned about keeping their communications private.

Tools for Data Loss Prevention (DLP): DLP tools assist businesses in monitoring and protecting sensitive data against illegal access and exfiltration.
Solutions for Identity and Access Management (IAM) Identity and access management (IAM) solutions control user access, ensuring that only authorized users may access critical data. IAM solutions control user access.
Tools that Preserve Your Privacy While Browsing: Tools such as the Tor Browser improve anonymity and privacy while using the internet.
The technology known as blockchain provides a decentralized and tamper-proof method to manage data, which can improve the data's overall security as well as its level of privacy.
Privacy-Centric Search Engines Make use of search engines like DuckDuckGo or StartPage, which do not keep a record of the websites you visit or the terms you search for.
Platforms for Secure File Sharing and Collaboration Tools such as Nextcloud and Tresorit provide secure functionality for file sharing and collaboration.
Security Information and Event Management (SIEM) Systems: SIEM systems monitor network traffic and alert businesses to potential security problems. SIEM stands for the acronym "security information and event management."

5. **Considerations of an Ethical Nature**
   There is a growing awareness of the significance of ethical considerations in data privacy. The processes that organizations use to obtain and utilize data have to be open and accessible to the public. They should also make sure that data is handled in an ethical manner and without any bias, especially when applying technologies like AI and machine learning.
6. **The Changing Landscape of Data Privacy**

The terrain surrounding the protection of personal information is always shifting. New technologies, such as homomorphic encryption and decentralized identification systems, are on the cusp of being available, and they will usher in a new era of data protection and privacy protection for individuals. In addition, the part that governments and other regulatory agencies play in determining data privacy will continue to be an important consideration.

6.3 Regulatory Frameworks and Compliance

Regulatory frameworks and compliance standards play a vital role in assuring ethical business operations, defending individual rights, and sustaining trust in the digital ecosystem in today's linked and data-driven world. As the global regulatory landscape continues to change, individuals and businesses alike are being forced to traverse an increasingly complex web of laws and standards in order to comply with legal requirements, safeguard sensitive information, and make positive contributions to an environment that is secure and ethical. In this in-depth investigation, we delve into the world of regulatory frameworks and compliance, analyzing their significance as well as the difficulties they present and the techniques that may be used to ensure their effective application.

1. **Compliance Is Built on Regulatory Frameworks as a Foundation**
   To govern many elements of corporate operations, including data processing, safety, and ethics, regulatory frameworks are sets of rules, guidelines, and standards that are issued by governments, industry bodies, or international organizations. Regulatory frameworks are also known as regulatory compliance frameworks. These frameworks offer organizations a systematic foundation to follow in order to verify that they are in conformity with applicable laws and ethical standards.
2. **The Importance of Being in Compliance with Regulations**
   Compliance with all applicable rules and regulations is a requirement that must be met in order to avoid breaking the law. Infractions can result in financial penalties, legal action, and damage to one's reputation.
   Compliance with relevant regulations, such as GDPR, CCPA, and HIPAA, is necessary for the protection of personal and sensitive data.
   Trust from consumers Compliance is a demonstration of an organization's dedication to safeguarding the interests of its consumers, which helps to build trust.
   Compliance lowers the likelihood of adverse legal and financial outcomes connected with non-compliance. This benefit of compliance is known as risk mitigation.
   Ethical Responsibility: It promotes ethical norms and ensures companies act ethically and transparently by guaranteeing that they are accountable.
3. **The Changing Nature of the Regulatory Landscape**
   The regulatory environment is always going through shifts and changes. The formation and evolution of rules are all influenced by emerging technologies, unfolding events on a global scale, and shifting attitudes among the general public. Significant regulatory revisions are being made in fields such as data privacy, cybersecurity, and environmental protection in response to the rapid advancements that have been made in technology.
4. **Regulatory Frameworks That Are Shared**
   General Data Protection Regulation (GDPR): The GDPR establishes the requirements for data protection for the European Union and has had an influence on data privacy policies globally.
   The Health Insurance Portability and Accountability Act (HIPAA) is a law that was passed to protect individuals' private health information (PHI) within the healthcare industry.
   The California Consumer Privacy Act (CCPA) is a piece of legislation that provides residents of California with increased control over their personal information.

ISO 27001: The International Standard for Information Security Management Systems ISO 27001 is an international standard.

PCI DSS stands for the Payment Card Industry Data Security Standard. This standard ensures that payment card data is handled securely.

The Sarbanes-Oxley Act (SOX) is a law that was passed to safeguard investors by regulating financial reporting and auditing processes.

5. **Obstacles to Becoming Compliant with Regulations**

The legal vocabulary and intricacy of many regulations can be intimidating, making it difficult for enterprises to properly grasp and apply all of the requirements.

Changing Environment: Organizations are required to continually modify their operations in order to remain compliant with both newly enacted regulations and updated versions of current regulations.

Compliance Across Borders: Businesses that operate in multiple countries must face the challenge of complying with a variety of national and regional regulations.

Allocation of Resources: Accomplishing compliance typically calls for a significant allocation of resources, which may include monetary investment, the training of staff, and technological changes.

Protecting sensitive data and ensuring that cybersecurity measures meet compliance standards can be challenging. Both of these tasks are important to ensure that data is kept private.

Ethical Considerations: Striking a balance between many ethical considerations, such as making responsible use of AI, can be difficult, particularly in sectors that rely heavily on data analytics.

6. **Methods for Achieving Successful Compliance with Regulations**

A proactive and strategic approach is required in order to successfully navigate the regulatory landscape and ensure compliance with its requirements.

Dedicated Compliance Officer: Appoint a compliance officer or team that will be responsible for monitoring any changes to the applicable regulations and ensuring that they are adhered to.

Assessment of Risk It is important to conduct risk assessments on a regular basis in order to identify areas in which compliance may be weak or at risk.

Education and Training: Invest in the education and training of your workforce to ensure that everyone is aware of their roles and responsibilities in upholding regulatory compliance.

Software for Compliance Make use of software for compliance management to automate operations, keep records, and generate compliance reports.

Tools for Data Privacy: Install data privacy tools and platforms to assist in the management and protection of sensitive information.

Audits and Assessments: On a regular basis, audit and assess the processes and

compliance of your organization in order to locate areas where there is room for development.
Collaboration Across Departments To ensure that a comprehensive approach to compliance is taken, it is important to encourage collaboration across a number of departments, including legal, IT, and HR.
Stakeholder Engagement In order to show that you are committed to compliance and ethics, you should engage with many stakeholders, including your consumers.
Continuous Monitoring: Put in place monitoring systems that run continuously in order to identify and address compliance issues as soon as they arise in real time.

7. **Adherence to Ethical Standards**
   In addition to complying with laws and regulations, ethical compliance is becoming an increasingly important factor. Compliance with ethical norms requires adhering to moral standards and ideals, even in spheres of activity for which there may not yet be any legislation. The relevance of ethical compliance as a means of fostering trust with stakeholders and society as a whole is becoming increasingly recognized by organizations.
8. **The Importance of Technology in the Regulatory Process**
   Software for Governance, Risk, and Compliance (abbreviated as GRC): This type of software assists businesses in managing risk and compliance in an integrated manner.
   Tools for the Management of Data Privacy: These tools assist organizations in managing data subject requests, consent, and the obligations for data protection.
   Solutions for Cybersecurity Robust cybersecurity precautions are an absolute necessity for ensuring compliance with applicable data protection legislation and standards.
   Artificial Intelligence and Machine Learning: Technologies using AI and machine learning can be used to assist in monitoring for compliance deviations and security threats.
9. **The Prospects for Regulatory Compliance in the Future**

Because of globalization, there will be a greater need to harmonize worldwide compliance requirements in order to accommodate the expansion of international commercial activities.

Data Privacy: The constantly changing legislation governing data privacy will continue to have an impact on the way in which enterprises manage personal and sensitive data.

AI and Automation: Technologies using AI and automation will play an increasingly important role in guaranteeing compliance and identifying deviations from the norm.

Compliance with Ethical Standards: In the future, ethical considerations will play an increasingly important role in compliance methods.

Regulations Regarding the Environment: Regulations regarding the environment will continue to develop as a direct response to concerns over climate change and sustainability.

Individuals and businesses alike have a continuous struggle when it comes to navigating the complicated terrain of regulatory frameworks and ensuring compliance with them. It is impossible to overestimate the significance of adhering to legal, ethical, and industry-specific standards since doing so assures responsible business operations, safeguards sensitive data, and helps to build confidence in a world that is always changing and increasingly interconnected. Organizations and individuals can successfully traverse the complicated regulatory landscape and develop a foundation of ethical and lawful behaviors by embracing technology, remaining informed about regulatory updates, and implementing effective compliance strategies. Additionally, staying educated about regulatory updates requires staying informed about regulatory changes.

6.4 Future Threats and Mitigation

The world is always changing, with developments in technology, increasing globalization, and shifting environmental conditions all having an impact on the path that our future will take. These advancements have the potential to bring about a wide variety of dangers, any one of which might have far-reaching repercussions for humanity. Despite the fact that they have brought about a great many advantages, they have also brought about a great many hazards.

The need for comprehensive mitigation methods is of the utmost importance if we are to achieve a future that is both sustainable and prosperous for future generations, given the difficulties that are posed by climate change and the depletion of resources, as well as the dangers that are linked with developing technologies and geopolitical conflicts.

The ever-worsening effects of climate change are quickly becoming one of the most important concerns for the foreseeable future. It is anticipated that as temperatures throughout the world continue to rise, sea levels will continue to rise, which will result in the relocation of millions of people who currently live in coastal locations. In addition, severe weather events like hurricanes, droughts, and wildfires are happening more frequently and with greater intensity, which is wreaking havoc on infrastructure, agriculture, and ecosystems. In order to lessen the impact of these dangers, nations will need to make lowering their emissions of greenhouse gases a top priority. This can be accomplished through the use of renewable energy sources, the promotion of reforestation efforts, and the development of sustainable urban planning.

In tandem with the effects of climate change, the diminishing availability of natural resources is a significant obstacle in the path toward the continued existence of human civilization. It is possible that overexploiting stocks of fossil fuels, minerals, and freshwater could result in a shortage of resources as well as potential conflicts over access to essential commodities. A transition toward circular economies that prioritize the conservation of resources and recycling is an essential component of any response to this challenge. Additionally, in order to lessen reliance on limited resources, it is necessary to make investments in research and development of alternative, environmentally friendly materials and technologies.

The lightning-fast progression of technology carries with it a plethora of new dangers that could potentially befall our future. Although it presents enormous prospects for innovation and growth, artificial intelligence (AI) also raises worries about employment displacement and the ethical difficulties surrounding autonomous decision-making. It is vital to have more stringent rules and the construction of ethical frameworks for the development and deployment of AI in order to make sure that these technologies are utilized in a responsible manner that also provides benefits to society. In addition, it is essential to make investments in education and training programs that provide individuals with the skills necessary to flourish in a workforce that is becoming increasingly automated in order to minimize the possible societal disruptions that could be created by advances in technology.

In the field of information technology security, the ever-increasing connectivity of digital systems exposes individuals and organizations to a variety of cyber risks, including data breaches, identity theft, and even cyber warfare. As our reliance on digital infrastructure continues to grow, it is more important than ever to implement stringent cybersecurity safeguards.

Enhanced coordination between governments, organizations, and cybersecurity professionals is required in order to establish comprehensive plans that protect sensitive data and vital infrastructure against destructive assaults. These strategies need to be implemented as soon as possible. In addition, the dissemination of information regarding digital literacy and awareness programs can enable users to adopt secure online practices, which in turn contributes to a digital ecosystem that is more robust and secure.

In addition, geopolitical tensions and wars provide a substantial risk to the continuity and security of the global system. The spread of nuclear weapons, ideological clashes, and territory disputes all continue to stoke the flames of uncertainty and the possibility for large-scale international catastrophes. It is absolutely necessary to make diplomatic efforts aimed at fostering cooperation, dialogue, and the resolution of issues in order to reduce the likelihood of armed conflicts and to promote global peace and stability. Multilateral agreements and organizations that promote diplomatic discourse and negotiation play an essential part in halting the escalation of crises and fostering international cooperation. This is because such agreements and institutions make it easier for countries to talk to one another and negotiate.

In addition to this, the recent pandemic and infectious disease outbreaks have brought to light the precarious state of the world's health care infrastructure in the face of future epidemics. Significant dangers to public health and well-being are posed by the appearance of newly discovered infections, the development of resistance to antimicrobials, and the lack of proper healthcare infrastructure. It is essential to make investments in public health infrastructure, disease surveillance systems, and research and development for innovative vaccines and treatments in order to adequately prepare for and mitigate the effects of potential future health crises. In order to effectively combat and stem the spread of infectious illnesses on a worldwide scale, it is vital to strengthen international collaboration and coordination among healthcare organizations and governments.

Chapter 7

Global Connectivity and 5G

The modern world is more connected to one another than any other time in history. Connectivity throughout the globe has emerged as a fundamental driver of change in the 21st century, impacting not just our economy but also our society and the way we go about our everyday lives. The fifth generation of mobile networks, often known as 5G, is one of the most important aspects of this change since it promises to take global connectivity to new heights. During this in-depth investigation, we will delve into the complex world of global connectivity, deconstruct the potential and impact of 5G, and investigate the difficulties and possibilities that lie ahead.

1. The Development of Worldwide Interconnectivity

Before we can begin to comprehend the importance of 5G, we need to examine the development of global connection from its infancy till the present day.

1. **The Inception of the World Wide Web**
   The advent of the Internet in the latter half of the 20th century marks the beginning of the path toward global connectedness. The Internet was initially conceived of as a research project; but, it swiftly expanded into a global information-sharing network, which significantly changed the way that we connect with one another, work, and access information. High-speed broadband internet replaced dial-up connections and simple web pages, paving the way for more advanced forms of media, online shopping, and social networking.
2. **The Development of 3G and 4G Networks**
   At the turn of the 21st century, 3G (third-generation) mobile networks were introduced, making mobile data accessible to the general public for the first time. This opened the door for mobile internet access of a more restricted nature, which in turn paved the way for vital services such as email and fundamental

web browsing on early smartphones. After that, the rollout of 4G (fourth-generation) networks brought about a significant improvement in both the rates of data transfer and the capacities of the networks, making it possible for streaming services, mobile applications, and the proliferation of smart gadgets.

3. **The Potential of the 5G Network**

Now, with the arrival of 5G, we are on the precipice of yet another revolution in technology. Fifth-generation networks are on the verge of delivering a quantum jump in global connectivity that has never been seen before. It is the goal of 5G to unleash the full potential of technologies such as the Internet of Things (IoT), augmented reality (AR), virtual reality (VR), driverless vehicles, and many more by delivering faster download and upload speeds, lower latency, and increased network capacity. This transformation will change industries, open up new chances for economic growth, and rethink how we engage with technology.

II. Having an Understanding of 5G

1. **Velocitiy and Latencies**

   The amazing speed that 5G can provide is one of its most notable characteristics. In contrast to the normal download rates offered by 4G networks, which range from 5 to 50 Mbps, it is anticipated that 5G would offer peak download speeds of up to 20 Gbps. Because of this enormous increase in speed, users will have the ability to download huge files more instantly, stream high-definition content more smoothly, and enjoy an overall more satisfying experience.

   In addition, the latency of 5G networks is expected to be substantially lower compared to that of their predecessors. The term "latency" refers to the amount of time that elapses between when data is generated and when it is received at its intended location. The normal latency for 4G networks is between 30 and 50 milliseconds, which is sufficient for the vast majority of applications. This delay, on the other hand, can be reduced to as little as 1 millisecond or less with 5G. In applications such as autonomous vehicles, remote surgery, and augmented reality, where it is important to transmit data in real time, this low latency is critical.

2. **An Increase in the Capacity of the Network**

   The amount of information that is required by more software and hardware means that there is a continuously expanding demand for it. 5G networks have been developed to accommodate this surge in data traffic by offering additional network capacity. These networks have been designed in order to accommodate the rollout of 5G. They accomplish this by utilizing higher frequency bands, which can transmit more data but only over a shorter distance than lower frequency bands. In addition to this, the installation of a wide network of tiny cells and the incorporation of various technologies such as massive MIMO (Multiple

Input, Multiple Output) would be carried out.

As a consequence, we now have a network that is able to support a large number of concurrently connected devices without sacrificing either its speed or its performance.

This feature is essential for the development of smart cities, which require a large number of Internet of Things devices, ranging from traffic lights to environmental sensors, to continuously transmit data.

3. **Slicing of the Network**

Network slicing is one of the revolutionary capabilities that 5G will bring to the table. The creation of many virtual networks on top of a single physical infrastructure can be accomplished by network operators through the use of network slicing. Every one of these virtual networks can be altered to be tailored to the particular requirements of a wide variety of applications and services. For instance, one network slice could be reserved exclusively for Internet of Things devices, whereas another could provide highly dependable and low-latency connectivity for mission-critical applications such as industrial automation.

This capacity opens up new opportunities for companies and sectors, as it enables them to subscribe to network slices that precisely meet their requirements. In addition to this, it guarantees that the 5G network will be able to effectively handle a diverse array of use cases, ranging from the mundane to the remarkable.

III. Repercussions for the Industries

1. **Communications and media outlets**

   Because it is primarily responsible for constructing and maintaining the infrastructure needed to support these new networks, the telecoms industry is at the forefront of the deployment of 5G technology. 5G will make it possible for telecommunications providers to provide services that are both quicker and more dependable, such as improved mobile internet and fixed wireless access.

   In addition, telecommunications companies have the opportunity to tap into new revenue streams by providing specialized services to other industries, such as apps for Industry 4.0 and smart city solutions, as well as private networks for commercial enterprises. These prospects are absolutely essential to fostering growth and enhancing competitiveness in the telecoms industry.

2. **Healthcare & Medical**

   The medical field stands to gain a substantial amount from the implementation of 5G technology. The delivery of medical care may undergo a radical transformation if network slicing were combined with high-speed and low-latency connectivity.

   It is becoming easier to perform telemedicine, remote monitoring of patients, and even telesurgery, which will ensure that medical services can reach more

remote places and improve the quality of care provided to patients.
In addition, the Internet of Medical Things (IoMT) has the potential to flourish on 5G networks, which will make it possible for medical devices to send real-time data in a secure manner. This breakthrough has the potential to lead to quicker diagnoses that are also more accurate, as well as improved results for patients.

3. **The Transportation and Automotive Industries**
The development of autonomous vehicles and technology that allows cars to be connected to the internet has caused a rapid evolution in the automobile sector. The success of these developments is dependent on the deployment of 5G networks. Because of their low latency and high connectivity speeds, they are able to facilitate real-time communication between moving vehicles and moving traffic infrastructure, which enables transportation systems to be safer and more efficient.
Communication between cars (vehicle-to-vehicle, or V2V), as well as between vehicles and other objects (vehicle-to-everything, or V2X), will be required for autonomous vehicles to successfully negotiate complicated traffic conditions. 5G networks are essential for V2V and V2X communication. Not only will this transition have an effect on the automotive industry, but it will also have an effect on urban planning and the decrease of both traffic congestion and accidents.
4. **Manufacturing and the Fourth Industrial Revolution**
Communication that is dependable and has a low latency is crucial to the functioning of Industry 4.0, which is defined by the incorporation of digital technology into the production processes. The connectivity requirements for real-time monitoring and management of industrial machines and processes can be met by networks operating at 5G speeds. In terms of the production operations, this leads to higher efficiency, decreased downtime, and cost savings.
Additionally, the arrival of 5G paves the way for the widespread implementation of collaborative robots (also known as cobots) in production facilities. Cobots like this can operate alongside human workers, increasing overall productivity while simultaneously lowering the likelihood of accidents occurring on the job.
5. **Artistic Expressions and the Press**

Because high-speed internet is now more readily available, the media and entertainment business has already experienced a tremendous amount of upheaval. Streaming video and the distribution of content will both experience significant improvements thanks to 5G. Users will appreciate experiences that are less choppy and more engaging, and 5G's reduced latency will be especially helpful for gaming and augmented/virtual reality apps.

In addition, the rollout of 5G will make it possible to distribute material in a more personalized manner because service providers will be able to customize content recommendations and advertising based on data collected in real time from user interactions. The client engagement and income generated by the media and entertainment industry both stand to benefit from this development.

IV. Obstacles and Causes for Concern

Although 5G has a great deal of promise, it is not without its share of difficulties and worries.

1. **Investments in Physical Infrastructure**
   The rollout of 5G networks will need a large investment in the underlying infrastructure. This includes modernizing any existing cell towers, constructing any necessary new infrastructure, and ensuring that all areas are covered. The expenditures that are associated with these attempts can be exorbitant, and it may take years to attain complete coverage with 5G technology, particularly in more rural and distant places.
2. **Safety and Confidentiality**
   Concerns about safety and privacy are brought up by the advent of 5G technology, just as they are by any other innovation that boosts connectivity. It has become an attractive target for assaults due to the increasing number of connected devices and the possibility that the network could be vulnerable. It is of the utmost importance to protect the confidentiality and security of data that is transferred across 5G networks, as any breaches could have far-reaching repercussions.
3. **The Distribution of Spectrum**
   Access to appropriate radio frequency spectrum is necessary for 5G in order for it to fulfill its promises. Effective allocation and management of the spectrum is the responsibility of regulatory agencies and national governments. The rivalry for spectrum can be fierce, and it can be difficult to strike a healthy balance between private business concerns and the needs of the general public.
4. **Concerns Regarding Health**

Concerns have been raised among members of the general public about the possible adverse impact that 5G technology could have on one's health, particularly with regard to its utilization of higher-frequency bands such as millimeter waves. Even if a great number of research and specialists agree that 5G technology is risk-free, some communities' fears regarding the possibility of adverse health effects have spurred discussions and protests.

V. The Terrain on a Global Scale

1. **Rivalry in International Politics**
   The fight to be the dominant player in the 5G space has expanded beyond the realms of technology and business and has now entered the realm of geopolitics as well. Both the United States and China have been at the forefront of the development of 5G, with both nations aiming to take the lead in the global landscape of 5G. Concerns regarding security and technological sovereignty, as well as the possibility of fragmentation in global telecommunications, have been brought up as a result of this rivalry.
2. **The Requirements of International Bodies**
   The development of international standards is necessary prior to the widespread adoption and implementation of 5G technology. The International Telecommunication Union (ITU) and the 3rd Generation Partnership Project (3GPP) are two organizations that play an important part in the process of establishing these standards. It is absolutely necessary to harmonize standards in order to guarantee that 5G will be a success on a worldwide scale.
3. **The Influence of the Economy on the World**

It is anticipated that the broad implementation of 5G networks will have a significant impact on economies all over the world. It has the potential to promote economic growth, as well as innovation and employment creation. According to projections provided by McKinsey & Company, 5G could add up to $13.2 trillion to the value of the global economy by the year 2035.

VI. The Path That Lies Ahead

1. **Creativity and the Introduction of New Applications**
   It is very likely that the introduction of 5G technology will kick off a wave of innovation, similar to the way in which the smartphone ushered in the creation of new businesses and industries. With connectivity that is quicker, more reliable, and has lower latency, we may anticipate a rise in the development of new applications and services that are currently inconceivable to us.
   Augmented reality (AR) and virtual reality (VR) are one area that has a significant amount of untapped potential. The speed and low latency that 5G networks can deliver will make it possible to have more immersive experiences in a variety of contexts, including gaming, remote collaboration, and training simulations. The concept of smart cities will continue to develop, leading to an increase in the number of data-driven services and linked gadgets that improve city life.
2. **Regulation and Policy**
   The deployment of 5G networks will call for legislation and policy frameworks that are transparent and receptive to changing needs. Governments have the responsibility of striking a balance between the imperatives of fostering

innovation and economic progress and the necessity to protect citizens' personal information and privacy. In addition to addressing concerns such as infrastructure development and the prevention of monopolistic behavior among network operators, regulations ought to concentrate on the allocation of spectrum.

3. **Closing the Gap in Digital Infrastructure**
   It is necessary, as 5G technology evolves, to ensure that the advantages are accessible to all people, regardless of geographical location or socioeconomic position. This accessibility must be ensured in order for the technology to be successful. The digital divide must be closed, and this can only be accomplished by aggressive efforts to expand 5G service to rural and underprivileged areas. It is imperative that governments, in conjunction with the business sector, work toward the goal of making 5G services available and affordable to all.
4. **Continuity of Existence**
   The rollout and operation of 5G networks should be carried out with an eye toward minimizing their impact on the environment. In order to lessen the impact that 5G will have on the environment, energy-efficient infrastructure and environmentally friendly technologies should be implemented. In addition, 5G can be utilized for activities such as monitoring the environment and helping to conservation efforts, making the world a more sustainable place.
5. **Awareness Among the Public**

Concerns and misinformation have been prevalent in the run-up to the launch of 5G networks, particularly with regard to potential adverse impacts on human health. To address these issues and guarantee that the general public is properly informed, it is essential to conduct public awareness campaigns and transparent communication on the part of industry stakeholders and governmental agencies.

Since the advent of the internet, global connectivity has come a long way, and the transition to 5G marks the next phase in the evolution of this technology. 5G has the ability to change industries, accelerate economic growth, and create a world that is more interconnected. Its promise of blazing speeds, low latency, and greater capacity are all factors that contribute to this potential.

Nevertheless, it is not devoid of difficulties in any way. To fully realize the potential of 5G technology, it will be essential to address the aforementioned challenges, which range from investments in infrastructure to worries about data security. In a world that is becoming more interconnected, 5G is not simply about higher download speeds or improved smartphone experiences; rather, it is about paving the way for a future in which there are no limits to innovation and in which global connectivity becomes an essential part of our everyday lives. The way forward will undoubtedly be riddled with difficulties, but the potential rewards will be substantial. The way in which we travel along this path will have an effect not just on the future of global connectivity but also on the world as we know it.

7.1 Bridging the Digital Divide

The concept of a "digital divide" is a major worry in this day and age, when digital technology affects every aspect of our lives, from education and healthcare to employment and civic involvement, among other spheres of human endeavor. This divide is referring to the unequal access that people have to digital technologies and the internet, which maintains inequities in opportunities, information, and quality of life. It is not enough to simply improve access to technology; closing the digital divide also needs to be done as a method of promoting social equity and including more people. During this in-depth investigation, we will investigate the many facets of the digital divide, its effects on individuals and communities, and the methods and policies that are necessary to make the world a more digitally inclusive place.

1. **The Digital Divide: An Obstacle Containing Multiple Facets**

1. **The Gap in Accessibility**
   The "access divide" is the most obvious aspect of the "digital divide." It refers to the disparate access that various people have to technological resources, including the internet. Rural and underserved areas in many regions of the world do not have access to broadband internet, and marginalized groups frequently face affordability constraints that prevent them from purchasing personal devices or subscribing to internet services.
2. **The Difference in Usage**
   The "usage divide" is one facet of the digital divide that is less obvious but yet equally important. Even in situations when people have access, there are still differences in the ways in which they use the internet. Others may have more advanced abilities and make full use of the resources that can be found on the internet, whilst some individuals may have low digital literacy, which makes them reluctant to participate in activities that take place online.
3. **The Gap Between Empowered Groups**
   The "empowerment divide" exists in addition to the "access and usage divide." This dimension illustrates the distinction between the ways in which individuals and communities make use of digital technologies to improve the quality of their lives. Those who are able to effectively use the internet are in a position to access educational resources, obtain career possibilities, and participate in social and political dialogue, whilst those who are unable to do so are at a clear disadvantage.
4. **Content Splitting Up**

The "content divide" refers to the disparity that exists between the quality and relevancy of the internet content that is accessible to certain categories of people. Even when people have access to the internet and are comfortable using it, they may still run into problems linked to the availability of content that is appropriate to their requirements. This is especially true for languages spoken by a minority and for interests that fall into a specialized category.

II. Repercussions for Individuals and Their Communities

1. **Instruction**
   The digital divide has significant repercussions for today's educational system. Students who do not have dependable access to the internet or digital devices will be at a disadvantage in their academic pursuits as teachers increasingly mix online learning and digital resources into traditional classrooms. This has a negative impact not only on their academic achievement but also on the educational disparities that already exist.
   The COVID-19 pandemic brought to light the critical need to bridge the digital divide in educational institutions. The abrupt transition to studying through remote means brought to light discrepancies in students' access to technology and the internet, which caused many kids to fall farther behind. It is imperative that this gap be closed in order to provide students from all backgrounds with the same opportunities to flourish academically.
2. **Opportunities for Employment and Economic Advancement**
   The digital gap has a profound impact on the chances for work and the mobility of the economy. In today's employment market, having digital abilities is frequently a need for many different types of jobs. When it comes to getting jobs that pay well, people who do not have access to the internet and who are not trained in digital skills are at a serious disadvantage. This contributes to the continuation of wealth disparity and impedes social mobility.
3. **The Healthcare Industry**
   Access to various forms of digital technology and the internet is becoming an increasingly important component of medical care. People living in underserved or rural locations have greater access to medical treatment because to the advent of telemedicine, which enables remote consultations and makes healthcare more readily available. People are unable to access these essential healthcare services and, as a result, their health is put at risk. However, the lack of critical digital infrastructure prevents this from happening.
4. **Participation in Civic Life**

The digital divide has a profound impact on a number of aspects of civic life and the democratic process, including participation in these areas. Those who do not have access to digital platforms run the risk of being excluded from fully participating in their communities as well as the democratic process. As governments and organizations become more reliant on digital platforms for the transmission of information, voting, and public discourse.

III. Methods for Eliminating the Gap Caused by Digital Technology

1. **The Construction of New Facilities**
   In order to bridge the access gap, governments and entities from the private sector need to invest in the expansion and improvement of digital infrastructure. This includes the construction of high-speed broadband networks, with a special focus on places that are currently unserved and rural. In addition, the proliferation of public Wi-Fi hotspots has the potential to assist in the filling in of communication gaps in urban areas.
2. **Programs for Improving Digital Literacy**
   Literacy in digital media is an essential component in bridging the gap between those who do not use computers and those who do. People of all ages and walks of life should be able to participate in comprehensive programs designed to improve their digital literacy. These programs should teach not only fundamental digital skills but also critical thinking, internet safety, and the capacity to differentiate between legitimate information and misinformation as well.
3. **Initiatives Regarding Affordability**
   Policymakers and internet service providers both need to investigate ways to lower costs for underserved populations if they want to address the affordability component of the access divide. This can be accomplished through the use of regulatory measures, community-based initiatives, and government subsidies that promote cheap internet package prices.
4. **Partnerships Between the Public and Private Sectors**
   Partnerships between the public sector and the corporate sector are extremely important in reducing the digital gap. By working together, government agencies, businesses in the private sector, and organizations in the not-for-profit sector can pool their resources and combine their areas of expertise to address the complex problems posed by the digital divide. These agreements have the potential to expand access to broadband internet, give training in digital literacy, and support local projects.
5. **Projects Involving the Community**
   At the grass-roots level, bridging the digital divide can frequently be accomplished most effectively through community-based efforts. Local organizations, schools, and libraries may play a crucial role in providing access to technology and the internet, as well as offering digital literacy programs that are adapted to meet the need of their respective communities.
6. **Inclusivity in the Progress of Technology**

The technology sector ought to make increased efforts toward increased inclusion in the creation of products and content. This necessitates the development of technology that can support a wide range of requirements, as well as the modification of online material to accommodate a variety of languages and cultural norms. A method of developing technology that is more open to participation could help reduce the content divide.

IV. The Prospects for Broader Digital Participation

As we look to the future, we must make it a global priority to ensure that everyone has access to digital technology. The potential benefits are enormous, including a global population that is better educated, more wealthier, and more actively engaged. It is absolutely necessary that initiatives to increase digital inclusion be maintained and adapted to the always developing technology and social dynamics.

1. **5G and Everything Beyond**
   The introduction of 5G network technology presents a chance to increase both access and connectivity. Access to the internet in more remote and rural regions can be made to be more dependable and faster thanks to these networks. However, it is necessary to guarantee that the rollout of 5G networks is fair and does not exacerbate existing inequalities before proceeding with the project.
2. **The Importance of Computer-Generated Intelligence**
   The use of artificial intelligence (AI) has the potential to significantly contribute to efforts aimed at expanding internet access. AI has the potential to assist in the development of individualized training programs for digital literacy, to facilitate the access of individuals with disabilities to digital resources, and to facilitate the translation and localization of text.
3. **Cooperation on a Global Scale**
   The digital gap is a worldwide concern, and if we are going to find a solution to it, we will need to work together with other countries. In order to advance digital inclusion on a global scale, governments, organizations that are not-for-profit, and firms in the technology sector need to collaborate in order to exchange best practices and resources.
4. **Measuring and Keeping an Eye on the Progress**

Establishing goals that can be measured and keeping track of progress is an essential step in ensuring that efforts to increase digital inclusion will be successful. It is necessary to gather and examine data regarding internet access, digital literacy, and the use of technology in order to evaluate the effectiveness of policies and programs.

To bridge the digital divide, it is not enough to simply distribute digital gadgets or provide internet access to those in underserved areas. It is about establishing a society that is more equal and inclusive, one in which every individual, regardless of their history or the circumstances of their life, has the opportunity to fully engage in the digital era. The integration of digital technology has a wide range of positive effects, including the advancement of education and healthcare, the expansion of economic prospects, and the consolidation of democratic procedures. It is very necessary for us to place a high priority on digital inclusion in order to guarantee that no one will be left behind in the quickly transforming digital landscape as technology continues to grow.

7.2 The Role of International Collaboration

In a world that is becoming more interconnected, the function that is played by international collaboration has become more important than it has ever been. Working together on a global scale has proven to be vital for solving difficult issues like climate change, global health crises, and economic instability. This is because nations are grappling with the same challenges at the same time, which range from climate change to global health crises.

In this piece, we will investigate the significance of international cooperation in the globalized world of today and analyze its influence on a variety of spheres, including politics, the economy, and national security, among others.

1. **Coordination on the Political Front**

   Facilitating Peace and the Resolution of Conflicts

   The upkeep of global peace and tranquility is directly related to the effectiveness of collaboration on a worldwide scale. Nations join together to discuss crises, settle disputes, and devise strategies for the prevention and resolution of conflicts through diplomatic forums and organizations such as the United Nations (UN) and the G7 and G20. These organizations and forums are known together as the "global community." These coordinated activities have the goals of preventing military crises, fostering diplomatic dialogue, and providing support for missions to keep the peace.

   One of the most prominent examples of this is the nuclear agreement with Iran, which is officially referred to as the Joint Comprehensive Plan of Action (JCPOA). The Joint Comprehensive Plan of Action (JCPOA) was a solution to the diplomatic impasse about Iran's nuclear program that was established through negotiations involving multiple states. Even though difficulties were encountered after the agreement was reached, it was a successful demonstration of the possibility for international cooperation to avert a crisis.

   Reduced Impacts of Climate Change

   The problem of climate change is intrinsically a global one due to the fact that the effects of environmental deterioration do not recognize national boundaries. By working together on a global scale through initiatives such as the Paris Agreement, governments are able to jointly establish objectives and divide duties related to the fight against climate change and the reduction of greenhouse gas emissions.

   Beyond the signing of accords, collaborative efforts to address climate change include supporting scientific research, technical innovation, and financial assistance for the purpose of assisting underdeveloped nations in adapting to the effects of climate change. The Global Environment Facility (GEF) and the

Green Climate Fund are two examples of international financial structures that are aimed to fund projects all over the globe that are related to climate change and sustainable development respectively.

2. **The Integration of the Economy**

Trade and Commercial Activity

The international cooperation and trade agreements are extremely important to the functioning of the global economy. Facilitating the establishment of rules and standards for international trade are organizations such as the World Trade Organization (WTO), which facilitates discussions. These agreements lower trade obstacles, which in turn encourages economic growth and opens up opportunities for enterprises to expand into new markets.

Regional trade agreements, such as the single market of the European Union or the North American Free Trade Agreement (NAFTA), which has since been succeeded by the United States-Mexico-Canada Agreement (USMCA), are examples of how countries can collaborate to boost economic integration and enhance their collective competitiveness. Other examples include the North American Free Trade Agreement (NAFTA), which has now been succeeded by the United States-Mexico-Canada Agreement (USMCA).

Financial Support for Development

The efforts of several countries to collaborate are extended through various programs of aid for development. The reduction of global inequities, the alleviation of poverty, and the promotion of sustainable development in less well-off countries are all made possible in large part by programs involving financial support, foreign aid, and capacity-building. In order to provide essential support to nations that are struggling, international organizations such as the United Nations Development Programme (UNDP) and the World Bank operate in conjunction with countries that make financial contributions.

In addition, the adoption of the 2030 Agenda for Sustainable Development by all of the states that are members of the United Nations displays worldwide cooperation in the fight against problems such as poverty, inequality, and the deterioration of the environment. A common aspiration for a brighter and more environmentally friendly future is encapsulated in the Sustainable Development Goals (SDGs).

3. **Safety and Defensive Measures**

The fight against terrorism

In order to effectively counteract the global terrorist threat, extensive international cooperation is required. Because terrorist networks frequently operate across international borders, it is vital for governments to share intelligence, coordinate security measures, and build collective strategies for countering terrorism. Cooperation in tackling the underlying causes of terrorism, avoiding radicalization, and strengthening security responses are the goals of several initiatives, such as the Global Counterterrorism Forum (GCTF), which aims to encourage such initiatives.

Protection against cyberattacks

Cyberattacks can come from anywhere in the world and are always getting more sophisticated. It is absolutely necessary to have international cooperation in the field of cybersecurity in order to defend critical infrastructure and fight cybercrime. Sharing threat intelligence, coordinating responses to cyberattacks, and adopting uniform cybersecurity standards and norms are all necessary steps towards achieving this goal. In order to improve international collaboration in the fight against cybercrime, organizations such as INTERPOL and the United Nations Office on Drugs and Crime (UNODC) are hard at work.

Interventions for Humanitarian Purposes and Maintaining Peace

The maintenance of peace and the response to humanitarian crises both benefit immensely from the participation of the international community. In order to accomplish its mission of preserving peace and security in zones of war, the United Nations employs troops and personnel from a variety of countries that collaborate closely with one another. These missions are only made possible because to the cooperation and assistance of a large number of states, which demonstrates the dedication of the international community to averting conflicts and protecting populations that are vulnerable.

4. **Health Care for the Public**

Initiatives for International Health

The COVID-19 pandemic brought to light the significance of the importance of worldwide collaboration in the field of public health. Because viruses and diseases do not respect national boundaries, it is essential for countries to work together to monitor, respond to, and contain pandemics. Sharing of information, coordination of vaccine delivery, and the establishment of standards for safe international travel are all examples of how organizations such as the World Health Organization (WHO) facilitate global responses to health emergencies.

Research in Medicine and the Development of Vaccines

Research conducted together by multiple scientists is essential to the advancement of medical knowledge. The creation of vaccines, the discovery of new drugs, and other advances in medical technology have been significantly aided by international collaboration among researchers, scientists, and pharmaceutical corporations. The speedy production and dissemination of vaccinations against COVID-19 illustrate the efficacy of international cooperation in the face of a public health emergency on a worldwide scale.

5. **Organizations Working on Multiple Fronts**

The United Nations Organization

The United Nations (UN), which was established in 1945, is still considered to be one of the most prominent manifestations of international cooperation. The United Nations (UN) is comprised of 193 member states and acts as a forum for diplomacy, the resolution of conflicts, and coordination on a broad variety of global concerns. These issues include everything from development and human rights to peace and security.

Both the World Bank and the International Monetary Fund (IMF)

The International Monetary Fund (IMF) and the World Bank are two organisations that are essential to the maintenance and growth of global financial markets. They do this by offering member countries financial assistance, advise on economic policy, and technical help, all with the goal of encouraging economic growth and stability.

Organization for the World Health (WHO)

The World Health agency (WHO) is the preeminent international agency that is accountable for world health. It plays an essential part in addressing public health emergencies, establishing health standards, and coordinating international responses to pandemics and other health crises around the world.

ICC stands for the International Criminal Court.

The International Criminal Court (ICC) is a global court that tries persons on international charges including genocide, crimes against humanity, crimes of aggression, and war crimes. It is a symbol of international cooperation in the pursuit of accountability for persons who have committed serious violations of international law.

When it comes to tackling the multifaceted and intertwined problems that our globalized society presents, international cooperation is absolutely essential. The capacity of nations to collaborate on issues as diverse as politics and economics, national security, public health, and many others has a significant bearing on the wellbeing of our planet and the trajectory of its future. Fostering collaborative efforts and establishing international alliances is not only an option in this age when global problems require global answers; rather, it is an obligation for a more inclusive, peaceful, and successful world. In this era, global problems require global solutions.

7.3 5G and Cloud in Developing Nations

As the globe prepares to enter the era of 5G technology, its effects can be felt across a wide range of industries and geographic areas. The use of 5G in poor countries is one area that offers particularly promising potential. These nations might be catapulted into the modern era thanks to the synergy between 5G and cloud technology, which would also stimulate economic growth, improved healthcare, and increased education. In this piece, we will investigate how 5G and cloud technologies meet in developing countries, focusing specifically on the potential and challenges that emerge as a result of this crossing.

1. **Creating Opportunities for Connectivity**

The introduction of 5G technology represents a significant advance in connection thanks to its low latency and fast data transmission speeds. 5G has the potential to completely transform the internet landscape in underdeveloped countries, which have historically struggled with slow or unreliable connections. The digital gap can be bridged and formerly underserved regions can be connected with the help of expanding 5G infrastructure, which allows for more people and communities to gain access to the internet.

Cloud computing is an extremely important component of this connectivity since it enables the storing and processing of data in remote data centers that can be accessed via the internet. Individuals and organizations in developing nations now have access to and the ability to exchange more data, applications, and services than ever before thanks to the convergence of 5G and cloud technology. This not only improves communication but also paves the way for a wide variety of applications across a number of different industries.

2. **Potential Career Paths in Healthcare**

   The combination of 5G and cloud technologies has enormous promise for enhancing the delivery of healthcare in countries still struggling to meet their basic needs. Telemedicine, for instance, becomes more readily available and efficient when 5G connectivity is available. Utilizing telehealth technologies, medical professionals are able to undertake sophisticated surgical procedures, hold remote consultations with patients, and check their states in real time.

   Cloud computing is an essential component in the process of safely storing and analyzing medical data, which in turn makes this information available to medical experts located all over the country. It is possible to handle electronic health records (EHRs) effectively in the cloud, which ensures that patient information is easily accessible whenever and wherever it is required.

   Furthermore, cloud-based diagnostic tools that are driven by artificial intelligence (AI) can help in the speedy and accurate diagnosis of diseases, especially in rural places that have limited access to healthcare facilities. It is possible for the combination of 5G and cloud technology to drastically cut down on healthcare inequities and greatly enhance overall health outcomes.

3. **Developments in the Field of Education**

   The combination of 5G and cloud technology has the potential to revolutionize the educational system in countries still on the path to economic growth. Connectivity to high-speed internet gives students and teachers unprecedented opportunities to access online materials, take part in virtual classrooms, and engage in learning activities that need collaboration on a scale never seen before. Students are able to access lectures, assignments, and interactive materials regardless of where they are physically located because the cloud offers the infrastructure necessary to store instructional content.

   The introduction of 5G and cloud computing has made the possibility of distance and online learning more practicable. Students who live in places that are underserved or rural can connect with their professors and peers, which helps to develop an education system that is more inclusive and equal. In addition, cloud-based educational platforms may adapt to the progress that students make and offer tailored learning experiences, which eventually leads to improved educational outcomes.

4. **The Progress of the Economy**
   Both 5G and cloud technology have the potential to serve as drivers of economic growth in developing countries. The cloud provides businesses with options that are both cost-effective and collaborative for the storage and distribution of software and data. The potential of cloud-based services may be leveraged by start-ups and smaller enterprises to help them grow their operations, increase their competitiveness on the global market, and provide new job opportunities. Businesses and entrepreneurs now have access to cloud-based software and services that are both rapid and efficient thanks to the advent of 5G connectivity. Computing in the cloud and fifth-generation wireless networks make it possible to analyze data in real time, which can result in improved decision-making and more effective use of resources. This is especially helpful in industries like agriculture, shipping, and manufacturing, which are all places where data-driven operations have the potential to increase production while simultaneously decreasing waste.
5. **Obstacles and Things to Take Into Account**

While there is significant promise for 5G and cloud technologies to improve the lives of people in underdeveloped countries, there are also a number of obstacles that must be overcome.

Investing in Infrastructure 5G networks and cloud data centers both require a considerable financial commitment in order to be deployed. The requisite infrastructure must be built, which may be an expensive and time-consuming endeavor that requires commitment from both public and private sector groups.

Affordability: It is crucial to make certain that individuals and organizations in developing nations have access to cloud solutions and 5G services at prices that are within their budgets. This may necessitate the use of regulatory measures, public-private partnerships, or subsidies in order to keep costs in check.

Literacy in Digital Spaces Access to cutting-edge technology alone is not sufficient; one must also possess proficiency in digital spaces. To ensure that individuals are able to make the most of the potential given by 5G and cloud technologies, it is necessary to develop programs for digital literacy and education.

The storage and transmission of data in the cloud must be encrypted to ensure users' privacy and the protection of their data. Developing countries have a responsibility to adopt stringent data protection rules and security measures in order to secure sensitive information.

Bridging the Digital Divide Although 5G and cloud technology have the ability to bridge the digital divide, it is necessary to focus on inclusivity and ensure that rural and underprivileged groups have access to these technologies. Only then will the digital divide truly be bridged.

The combination of 5G and cloud technology opens up a vast array of possibilities for countries still on the path to economic growth. The effects of this synergy are extremely far-reaching, ranging from the enhancement of healthcare and education to the growth of the economy and the improvement of connections. However, in order to realize the full promise of 5G and cloud technology in these locations, it is essential to solve the difficulties connected with infrastructure, cost, digital literacy, security, and inclusion.

The facilitation of the implementation of 5G networks and cloud infrastructure in developing nations can also be greatly aided by international collaboration and collaborations with technology businesses and organizations. Developing countries have the potential to harness the power of connection to leapfrog into a more wealthy and equitable future if they make investments in these transformative technologies and overcome the hurdles associated with those investments.

7.4 The Geopolitical Landscape of Telecommunications

Because it is such an important and rapidly developing industry, geopolitics has always been intricately entwined with telecommunications. Because of its capacity to connect nations and to mold economies, technology is a potent instrument for exerting influence on a global scale. The geopolitical landscape of telecommunications is undergoing substantial alterations in the 21st century as countries compete for control, influence, and security in this crucial domain. These shifts are being brought about by the globalization of the industry. The dynamics, problems, and strategies that are defining the contemporary geopolitical environment of telecommunications are discussed in this article.

1. **The Significance to Strategy**
   The infrastructure that supports modern global communication and business is the telecommunications industry. This infrastructure includes wired and wireless networks, satellites, and underwater cables. It makes international voice and data transfer, as well as cross-border trade and the movement of information, easier to accomplish. Countries who are striving to increase their influence on the international scene have taken note of the strategic significance of this issue.
2. **The Ability to Lead in Technology**
   Technological leadership is the driving force behind the geopolitics of the telecommunications industry. Power in both the economic and political spheres can be derived from one's capacity to develop and implement cutting-edge technologies. Throughout the course of history, the United States of America, China, and a select number of European nations have been considered to be

leaders in the field of telecommunications technology. However, a huge shift has occurred as a result of China's meteoric ascent in this field in recent years. Companies such as Huawei have quickly risen to the top of the worldwide market for telecommunications equipment, sparking discussions about the implications of their technological superiority for national security.

3. **Cybersecurity and its Relation to National Security**

   The proliferation of digital networks has made governments more vulnerable to new kinds of security threats. Cybersecurity is of the utmost importance because of the prevalence of potential cyberattacks and the susceptibility of essential infrastructure, such as power grids and financial systems, to assault via digital means. Because of this, geopolitical disputes frequently take the form of accusations and counteraccusations of state-sponsored cyberattacks, which further intertwines politics and technology.

   A particular area of concern is the infrastructure of telecommunications. Concerns have been raised over the potential for espionage, the theft of sensitive data, and the interruption of vital services as a result of both the management of network equipment and the presence of international technology companies in national networks.

   These worries are especially pertinent in the context of the development of 5G networks, in which nations are hesitant to grant access to their vital telecommunications infrastructure to corporations based in other nations for fear of compromising national security.

4. **Dominance in the Supply Chain**

   One of the most important geopolitical battlegrounds is the supply chain for telecommunications equipment. The manufacture and distribution of essential components, such as semiconductors and network infrastructure, are two areas that countries strive to control and dominate. It is a matter of both national and economic security for governments to maintain control over their supply chains, which allows them to exert influence over the deployment and protection of their telecommunications networks.

   For instance, the United States has utilized its export control regime to place restrictions on the sale of specific technologies to China and other countries, while at the same time actively promoting alternatives that are produced by American enterprises. Because of this, tensions have arisen in international trade and the dynamics of supply chains.

5. **Privacy of Information and Sovereignty of Data**

   The question of data privacy and sovereignty has recently arisen as a critical component of the

   geopolitical environment of the telecommunications industry. Data is a resource that is extremely important, and as a result, nations are increasingly taking steps to ensure that they have control over the data that is produced within their borders. The General Data Protection Regulation (GDPR) in Europe is one example of an attempt to preserve data privacy by placing severe regulations on how firms handle personal data. Other examples include the California Consumer Privacy Act and the California Transparency in Financial Transactions Act.

Because it involves the storing of data and the transfer of that data across national lines, this topic is closely related to the field of telecommunications. A growing number of nations are passing legislation known as "data localization laws," which stipulate that data must be kept inside their own borders. This has repercussions for platforms such as social networking, cloud services, and other types of digital communication.

6. **Financial and Business Concerns**

   Additionally, the field of telecommunications carries significant commercial interests. Companies operating in this industry are frequently multinational behemoths that exert a large degree of control over the state of an economy. The prosperity and expansion of businesses such as AT&T, China Mobile, and Vodafone have significant repercussions for the economies of the countries in which they are headquartered.

   In addition, these businesses are involved in a variety of international activities, including mergers and acquisitions, investments in undersea cables, and partnerships with providers of international telecommunications services. These financial facets frequently interweave with diplomatic relations and can have far-reaching effects on geopolitical dynamics.

7. **Power on the International Stage**

   The expansion of a nation's sphere of influence on the global stage can be facilitated by the utilization of various communications technologies. They do this through the establishment of international broadcasting networks, the promotion of their languages and culture through the media, and the engagement in soft power efforts. This competition for information and influence can evolve to "information warfare," which is when countries compete with one another for control of the information space on a global scale.

8. **Regulatory Frameworks**

   The governance of telecommunications is intricately entangled with international relations and geopolitics. National regulatory authorities are responsible for dictating how networks function within their respective boundaries, while international organizations such as the International Telecommunication Union (ITU) contribute to the establishment of global standards and rules. Countries wield power over these frameworks in order to further their own interests, whether those goals lie in gaining access to markets, ensuring their own safety, or exercising authority over essential infrastructure.

9. **Obstacles to Overcome and Working Together**

There are a lot of obstacles to overcome in the geopolitical landscape of the telecoms industry. The competition for supply chain dominance, as well as the tensions that exist between the United States and China, the disputes regarding the security of 5G, and so on, all present important challenges. Finding a happy medium between protecting the nation's security and advancing economic interests is an ongoing struggle.

At the same time, worldwide cooperation is required in order to effectively address global issues such as cyber threats, data privacy, and international standards. Countries need to cooperate together to define norms for responsible state behavior in cyberspace, establish guidelines for the responsible use of technology, and harmonize data protection policies.

The geopolitical environment of the world's telecommunications networks is becoming more intricate and influential by the day. Because of the numerous ways in which it intersects with technology, national security, economic interests, and information influence, it has become an essential arena for international rivalry and collaboration. The necessity for governments all over the world to strike a balance between the benefits of international communication and trade and the requirements of maintaining their security and sovereignty is an urgent concern.

The geopolitics of the field of telecommunications will surely continue to be an essential component of international politics and diplomacy even as the field of telecommunications technology continues to advance.

Chapter 8

The Future of Telecommunications

Since the dawn of civilization, people have relied on various methods to communicate with one another over great distances. One of these methods is known as telecommunications. The development of telecommunications, beginning with the telegraph and continuing with the advent of the internet, has had a significant impact on the ways in which we communicate, perform our jobs, and live our lives. With developments such as 5G, the Internet of Things (IoT), and quantum communication on the horizon, the foreseeable future of telecommunications promises to be even more revolutionary than it already is. In the course of this in-depth investigation, we are going to look into the technological tendencies, difficulties, and possibilities that will define the future of communications.

1. **The Opening Statements**
   The foundation of the digital age is found in the field of telecommunications. It comprises a wide variety of technologies, including wired and wireless communication, the internet, and satellite networks, all of which play vital roles in connecting individuals, businesses, and nations to one another. It is not simply about greater data speeds or more efficient networks in the future of telecommunications; rather, it is about rethinking how we engage with one another, how we work, and how we see the world.
2. **The Role of Emerging Technologies in Shaping the Future**
1. **5G and Everything Beyond**
   The Technology of 5G
   The launch of 5G networks will be one of the most important steps toward the evolution of the telecoms industry in the coming decades. Fifth-generation wireless technology, also known as 5G, enables higher data transfer rates, lower latency, and the simultaneous connection of a greater number of devices. These advancements are going to cause a revolution in a variety of different areas,

ranging from healthcare and transportation to entertainment and intelligent cities.

Streaming in ultra-high resolution, experiences in augmented and virtual reality, and the transmission of enormous data volumes in real time will all be made possible by 5G. In addition to this, it will assist in the expansion of the Internet of Things (IoT) by delivering the dependable and responsive connectivity that is necessary for a world that is becoming increasingly interconnected.

IoT stands for "the Internet of Things"

The Internet of Things represents a paradigm shift in the field of telecommunications. Connecting a plethora of different devices, ranging from smart home appliances and wearables to industrial sensors and autonomous vehicles, is a necessary step in the process. These gadgets will be able to communicate with one another and with central systems, which will result in the generation of large volumes of data that can be utilized for a variety of purposes.

The Internet of Things will have a significant impact on a variety of sectors in the future, including healthcare, agriculture, transportation, and manufacturing. For instance, medical professionals will use wearable technology to perform remote patient monitoring, while farmers will maximize crop management by utilizing soil sensors and drones as part of smart agriculture.

2. **Computing at the Edge**

   Computing at the network's edge is positioned to assume a leadership position in the field of telecommunications in the not-too-distant future. Instead than depending entirely on centralized cloud data centers, this paradigm involves processing data at the "edge" of the network, which is located closer to the source of the data. Edge computing provides real-time applications and improves the performance of Internet of Things devices. This is accomplished by lowering latency and improving response times.

   Applications of edge computing are quite diverse, ranging from autonomous vehicles, which must make decisions in a fraction of a second, to industrial processes, which must adhere to strict latency requirements. Additionally, it improves the experience of both augmented and virtual reality, which in turn makes gaming and remote collaboration more engaging.

3. **Communication on the Quantum Level**

The introduction of quantum communication signals a sea change in the approach taken to the

security of telecommunications. Due to the fact that it utilizes the fundamentals of quantum mechanics in order to encrypt and decrypt data, quantum key distribution (QKD) provides a level of security that is, in theory, impossible to breach. This technology has the ability to completely change the way that sensitive information is transmitted in areas such as the healthcare industry, government, and the financial sector.

Quantum communication, despite the fact that it is only in its infancy, is progressing quickly and shows promise for the future of secure data transmission. Research and development in the field of quantum communication is receiving funding from governments and organizations all around the world.

III. Obstacles that Loom in the Future

1. **Safety and Confidentiality**
   Significant security and privacy issues have been raised as a result of the proliferation of gadgets that may connect to the internet and the transmission of sensitive data across telecommunications networks. The hazards connected with cyberattacks, data breaches, and the compromise of vital infrastructure grow as our reliance on technological solutions increases. Maintaining the highest possible level of confidentiality and protection for telecommunications networks will continue to be a primary focus.
2. **Investments in the Infrastructure**
   Significant expenditures are necessary for the rollout of 5G networks and the extension of telecommunications infrastructure, particularly in areas that are not currently adequately covered. It is necessary for governments and companies that supply telecommunications services to work together in order to make sure that the benefits of sophisticated telecommunications are available to everyone, regardless of where they live or their socioeconomic standing.
3. **Obstacles in the Form of Regulations and Policies**
   In order to keep up with the rapid changes in the field of telecommunications technology, regulatory and policy frameworks need to undergo constant revision. In order to establish an atmosphere that is both just and safe for the use of telecommunications, it will be necessary to continue paying attention to and making modifications regarding issues such as the allocation of spectrum, the security of data, and the level of competition within the industry.
4. **Impact on the Environment**

The growth of data centers and other devices used for communication can have a substantial negative effect on the surrounding environment. Consumption of energy, proper disposal of electronic trash, and the amount of carbon dioxide emissions produced by data centers are all issues that need to be resolved before telecommunications technology can be considered sustainable and ecologically responsible.

IV. The Potential Uses of Communications Technology in the Future

1. **Intelligent Cities**
   The expansion of telecommunications infrastructure will be an essential component in the development of smart cities. Cities will be able to become more efficient, sustainable, and responsive to the demands of their citizens if they

integrate 5G, Internet of Things, and edge computing technologies. Applications like as intelligent transportation, energy management, and waste disposal will be among the most important factors in determining the character of the cities of the future.

2. **Healthcare & Medical**
   The delivery of medical treatment will evolve as a result of technological advances in telecommunications. The use of telemedicine, the monitoring of patients remotely using remote monitoring technology, and the sharing of medical data in real time will make healthcare more accessible and efficient. In addition, the introduction of 5G and edge computing will pave the way for the production of cutting-edge medical equipment as well as the speedy transmission of medical imaging data.
3. **The Education System**
   The world of education is heading in the direction of being increasingly digital and linked. The way in which students are taught will be fundamentally altered as a result of the convergence of augmented reality, virtual reality, and high-speed internet. Education delivered in a manner that is both remote and individualized will gain popularity, making it more likely that individuals, irrespective of where they live, will have access to educational opportunities of a sufficient standard.
4. **Mixed Realities (Augmented and Virtual)**

Experiences in augmented and virtual reality are about to undergo a sea change as a result of the convergence of 5G and edge computing. AR and VR will become more accessible, responsive, and realistic as a result of advancements in telecommunications technology. Examples of these advancements include immersive gaming, virtual travel experiences, and remote collaboration.

The future of telecommunications is both exciting and dynamic, and it will be defined by technical developments that will completely reimagine the ways in which we live and engage with one another. The potential for innovation are endless now that 5G, the internet of things (IoT), edge computing, and quantum communication are on the horizon.

Nevertheless, these potential come with a host of challenges, such as concerns around security and investment in infrastructure, as well as legal considerations.

It will be necessary for governments, corporations, and individuals to work together to exploit the full potential of these technologies while ensuring that their use is responsible and secure as the landscape of telecommunications continues to transform. It's not just about staying connected in the future of telecoms; it's also about how we can shape the world we live in and the experiences we have.

8.1 Emerging Technologies and Trends

The 21st century can be characterized by the lightning-fast pace at which technological advancements have been made. As we progress farther into this century, there are a number of developing technologies and trends that are on the verge of revolutionizing a variety of elements of our lives. These technologies are not only redefining industries but also how people connect with one another, work, and engage with the world around us. In this investigation of 1000 words, we will look into some of the most promising new technologies and trends that are driving forward progress and altering the globe.

1. **AI and ML (machine learning and artificial intelligence)**
   It's no exaggeration to say that artificial intelligence (AI) and machine learning are two of the most game-changing technologies of our time. AI systems that are outfitted with machine learning algorithms have the ability to independently examine enormous datasets, recognize patterns, and come to choices without human intervention. These technologies are currently being implemented in a wide variety of applications, ranging from diagnostics in the medical field to self-driving vehicles.
   The invention of deep learning models, such as deep neural networks, is one of the most interesting discoveries in the field of artificial intelligence (AI). These models are capable of doing tasks such as picture and speech recognition that were previously thought to be difficult for robots to accomplish. The application of AI in healthcare is particularly promising, as AI-driven diagnostic technologies are getting more accurate and trustworthy, with the potential to save lives through the early detection of disease.
2. **Computing on the Quantum Level**
   The field of computing is on the cusp of seeing a paradigm shift because to the arrival of quantum computing. Quantum computers, as opposed to classical computers, which rely on bits to process data, use qubits, which, according to the principles of quantum superposition and entanglement, are able to exist in several states simultaneously. Classical computers rely on bits. As a result, quantum computers are now capable of carrying out complicated calculations at rates that were previously inconceivable.
   Computing on the quantum level has the potential to transform a variety of industries, including cryptography, the search for new drugs, and challenges involving optimization. For example, it can have a huge influence on cybersecurity by deciphering encryption codes that were previously thought to be unbreakable. Companies such as IBM and Google, in addition to startups such as Rigetti, are making significant headway in the development of viable quantum computers.
3. **The Technology of 5G**
   The fifth-generation wireless technology, known as 5G, is currently being rolled out over the world. This new technology promises much higher data transfer speeds, reduced latency, and the capacity to connect more devices at the same

time. Many other industries are undergoing transformations as a result of the broad use of 5G, including telemedicine, driverless vehicles, and more.

The fifth-generation wireless (5G) technology is a critical enabler for the Internet of Things (IoT), which will connect billions of devices for use in smart cities, homes, and industries. This high-speed network will pave the way for applications of augmented and virtual reality, which will enhance the way in which we engage with digital content and the world around us.

4. **IoT stands for the Internet of Things.**

   The Internet of Things is a network of objects that are connected to one another. These devices might range from industrial machinery to smart thermostats and wearables. The Internet of Things has the potential to completely change the way we live and work by offering data in real time and control over a variety of different devices.

   In the field of healthcare, for instance, Internet of Things devices can keep track of the state of patients' health and relay critical information to medical professionals, thereby enabling remote monitoring and prompt intervention. Sensors that are connected to the internet of things can improve public safety, help control traffic flow, and cut down on energy use in smart cities.

5. **Both Biotechnology and Genetic Engineering are Used Here**

   Astonishing strides are being made in the field of biotechnology, which has the potential to provide solutions to some of the most critical issues facing our society today. These issues include healthcare, food security, and environmental sustainability. Scientists now have the ability to tweak genes and perhaps treat hereditary illnesses thanks to the development of techniques such as CRISPR-Cas9, which opened the door to precise genetic editing.

   Genetically modified crops have the potential to increase crop production, boost plants' natural resistance to harmful organisms, and better respond to shifting weather patterns. In addition, biotechnology is opening the way for customized medicine, which involves adapting medications to the unique genetic make-up of each patient in order to improve the success rate of treatments.

6. **Both Augmented Reality (AR) and Virtual Reality (VR) are types of mixed reality.**

   The technologies of augmented reality and virtual reality are causing a revolution in the way we experience and interact with the digital environment. The difference between augmented reality and virtual reality is that the former adds digital information to the real world, so enhancing our view of it, while the latter immerses users in totally digital surroundings.

   In the realm of education, virtual reality is making it feasible to take students on virtual field trips or to recreate complex scientific experiments. This results in a learning experience that is both more engaging and more immersive for the student. Virtual reality (VR) is providing more realistic and engaging gaming experiences in the gaming industry. This is blurring the border between the real world and the virtual world.

7. **Technologies Like Robotics and Automation**
   The advancement of robots and automation is causing a change in the ways in which we work, produce goods, and interact with the world around us. Manufacturing, logistics, and healthcare are just some of the fields that are rapidly turning to the employment of robots to carry out activities that need high levels of precision and efficiency.
   In distribution centers, autonomous robots are improving the procedures of order fulfillment, and in hospitals and other medical facilities, robotic-assisted surgeries are becoming increasingly common. These surgeries offer greater precision and faster recovery times. Another key use of robotics and automation is the development of self-driving automobiles, which companies like Tesla and Waymo are now leading the charge in.
8. **Technologies for Renewable and Sustainable Energy**
   The development of technologies that utilize renewable sources of energy has risen to the forefront as concerns about climate change and the long-term health of the environment continue to intensify. Solar and wind power have recently seen significant improvements in both their cost-effectiveness and their efficiency, which has elevated their status as potential replacements for conventional fossil fuels.
   Energy storage technologies are also advancing at a rapid rate, which enables the storing of excess renewable energy for use during periods of high demand. This is in addition to the significant advancements being made in the generation of power. Battery technology are getting better, and as a result, lithium-ion batteries are getting more powerful and more economical. This will make it possible to have electric vehicles and to store energy on a grid scale.
9. **Blockchain technology and virtual currencies**
   The blockchain technology was first intended to back cryptocurrencies like Bitcoin; however, it has now found uses in a variety of industries. It provides a decentralized and secure mechanism to record transactions, which makes it valuable in fields such as the administration of supply chains, banking, and healthcare, among others.
   The way we think about conventional currencies and the financial institutions that support them is evolving as a direct result of the rise of cryptocurrencies such as Bitcoin and Ethereum. They provide a borderless and decentralized means of moving and storing value, and they have the potential to disrupt traditional banking as well as the financial sector.
10. **Exploration of Space and the Commercialization of Space**
    Recent developments in space technology have made new avenues available for both the scientific investigation of space and the establishment of space-based

businesses. Private firms such as SpaceX and Blue Origin are pushing the limits of space travel with the intention of bringing down the cost of entering space and eventually making it available to a wider variety of people.

Private enterprises, in addition to government agencies, are interested in the mining of asteroids for valuable resources, the expansion of tourism into space, and even the establishment of colonies on other planets, such as Mars. Space exploration is not restricted to government entities only. These recent advancements are broadening our understanding of the cosmos, and they might have significant repercussions for the future of humanity.

11. **Printing in three dimensions (3D) and additive manufacturing (AM)**

    The process of additive manufacturing, also known as 3D printing, is a technology that enables the production of three-dimensional things through the layering of material, most frequently metal or plastic. This technology has a variety of uses, ranging from the aerospace industry to the healthcare industry.

    3D printing is utilized in the aircraft industry to make lightweight and complicated parts that would otherwise be difficult or impossible to fabricate.

    It is utilized in the medical industry for the production of individualized implants, prosthetics, and even human tissue for transplantation purposes. The ability to print things on demand is causing a shift in the way that products are designed and manufactured.

12. **Verification of identities using biometric identifiers**

    The use of biometric technology, such as fingerprint and facial recognition, is becoming increasingly integrated into a variety of aspects of our lives, ranging from the ability to unlock devices to the improvement of security systems. These technologies provide a means of verifying identities that is both more secure and more convenient.

    The use of biometrics in banking and other financial institutions has made safe authentication more feasible, hence lowering the danger of identity theft and fraud. Airports and other government organizations responsible for border control also use biometrics in order to improve the efficiency of border control and security processes.

13. **Computing on the Edge**

    Instead of depending on centralized cloud servers, a distributed computing paradigm known as edge computing processes data in locations physically closer to the point of origin where the data was generated. This results in a decrease in latency and enables faster data processing as well as decision-making in real time. Edge computing is especially useful for applications like autonomous vehicles and smart cities that have strict limits on the amount of delay they can tolerate. It is able to interpret data from sensors and devices quickly, which enables it to provide rapid response and decision-making in potentially life-threatening situations.

14. **Materials that are both biodegradable and friendly to the environment**
    The movement toward environmental sustainability has been a driving force behind technological advancements in the field of materials science. Traditional plastics and other materials that are damaging to the environment are being phased out in favor of newly created biodegradable and environmentally friendly technologies.
    Bioplastics, for example, are designed to naturally disintegrate and may be produced from renewable resources. This helps to reduce the amount of pollution that is released into the environment. These materials are finding uses in a variety of industries, including agriculture, consumer goods, and packaging.
15. **The Field of Cognitive Computing**
    The term "cognitive computing" refers to the practice of utilizing computer systems that are able to replicate the way humans think. Because of their ability to comprehend, reason, and learn from data, these systems are particularly beneficial in domains such as healthcare and customer service.
    In the field of medicine, cognitive computing systems can examine medical records and scholarly material to provide assistance in making diagnoses and decisions regarding treatments. Chatbots and virtual assistants that are powered by cognitive computing can provide tailored support and assistance to customers in the field of customer service.
16. **Technologies for Cybersecurity and Personal Privacy**
    The level of sophistication of cyberattacks is growing in tandem with the advancement of technology. The cybersecurity and privacy solutions that are used to safeguard individuals and businesses from cyberattacks and data breaches are constantly being developed and improved.
    The use of artificial intelligence in cybersecurity is becoming increasingly important as a means of detecting and neutralizing threats in real time. Encryption technologies are growing increasingly powerful, which ensures the confidentiality and safety of stored data. Blockchain is also being utilized for the purpose of storing records in a way that is both safe and transparent. This helps to prevent unwanted access to data as well as data tampering.
17. **The Field of Synthetic Biology**
    The practice of synthetic biology entails the planning and creation of biological parts, systems, and creatures that do not occur in nature. It has the ability to generate organisms that are specifically tailored for a variety of uses, such as biomanufacturing and environmental remediation, among others.
    Synthetic biology has the potential to be utilized in biomanufacturing, which involves the production of biofuels, medicines, and other important substances. In addition, it can help solve environmental problems by fostering the growth of organisms that can degrade contaminants and improve the state of the soil.

18. **Technology that can be worn**
 The use of wearable technology, such as smartwatches, fitness trackers, and glasses that display augmented reality, is becoming increasingly commonplace in our society. These gadgets have the ability to monitor various health measures, supply information in real time, and improve our connectivity.
 The use of fitness trackers, for example, which can monitor an individual's physical activity, heart rate, and sleep habits, can assist individuals in making more educated decisions regarding their health. By allowing users to get notifications and provide access to apps, smartwatches provide a convenient alternative to the widespread usage of smartphones in daily life.
19. **Verification of identities using biometric identifiers**
 The use of biometric technology, such as fingerprint and facial recognition, is becoming increasingly integrated into a variety of aspects of our lives, ranging from the ability to unlock devices to the improvement of security systems. These technologies provide a means of verifying identities that is both more secure and more convenient.
 The use of biometrics in banking and other financial institutions has made safe authentication more feasible, hence lowering the danger of identity theft and fraud. Airports and other government organizations responsible for border control also use biometrics in order to improve the efficiency of border control and security processes.
20. **Blockchain technology and virtual currencies**
 The blockchain technology was first intended to back cryptocurrencies like Bitcoin; however, it has now found uses in a variety of industries. It provides a decentralized and secure mechanism to record transactions, which makes it valuable in fields such as the administration of supply chains, banking, and healthcare, among others.
 The way we think about conventional currencies and the financial institutions that support them is evolving as a direct result of the rise of cryptocurrencies such as Bitcoin and Ethereum. They provide a borderless and decentralized means of moving and storing value, and they have the potential to disrupt traditional banking as well as the financial sector.
21. **Exploration of Space and the Commercialization of Space**
 Recent developments in space technology have made new avenues available for both the scientific investigation of space and the establishment of space-based businesses. Private firms such as SpaceX and Blue Origin are pushing the limits of space travel with the intention of bringing down the cost of entering space and eventually making it available to a wider variety of people.
 Private enterprises, in addition to government agencies, are interested in the mining of asteroids for valuable resources, the expansion of tourism into space, and even the establishment of colonies on other planets, such as Mars. Space

exploration is not restricted to government entities only. These recent advancements are broadening our understanding of the cosmos, and they might have significant repercussions for the future of humanity.

22. **Printing in three dimensions (3D) and additive manufacturing (AM)**
    The process of additive manufacturing, also known as 3D printing, is a technology that enables the production of three-dimensional things through the layering of material, most frequently metal or plastic. This technology has a variety of uses, ranging from the aerospace industry to the healthcare industry.
    3D printing is utilized in the aircraft industry to make lightweight and complicated parts that would otherwise be difficult or impossible to fabricate. It is utilized in the medical industry for the production of individualized implants, prosthetics, and even human tissue for transplantation purposes. The ability to print things on demand is causing a shift in the way that products are designed and manufactured.
23. **Verification of identities using biometric identifiers**
    The use of biometric technology, such as fingerprint and facial recognition, is becoming increasingly integrated into a variety of aspects of our lives, ranging from the ability to unlock devices to the improvement of security systems. These technologies provide a means of verifying identities that is both more secure and more convenient.
    The use of biometrics in banking and other financial institutions has made safe authentication more feasible, hence lowering the danger of identity theft and fraud. Airports and other government organizations responsible for border control also use biometrics in order to improve the efficiency of border control and security processes.
24. **Blockchain technology and virtual currencies**
    The blockchain technology was first intended to back cryptocurrencies like Bitcoin; however, it has now found uses in a variety of industries. It provides a decentralized and secure mechanism to record transactions, which makes it valuable in fields such as the administration of supply chains, banking, and healthcare, among others.
    The way we think about conventional currencies and the financial institutions that support them is evolving as a direct result of the rise of cryptocurrencies such as Bitcoin and Ethereum. They provide a borderless and decentralized means of moving and storing value, and they have the potential to disrupt traditional banking as well as the financial sector.
25. **Exploration of Space and the Commercialization of Space**

Recent developments in space technology have made new avenues available for both the scientific investigation of space and the establishment of space-based businesses. Private firms such as SpaceX and Blue Origin are pushing the limits of space travel with the intention of bringing down the cost of entering space and eventually making it available to a wider variety of people.

Private enterprises, in addition to government agencies, are interested in the mining of asteroids for valuable resources, the expansion of tourism into space, and even the establishment of colonies on other planets, such as Mars. Space exploration is not restricted to government entities only. These recent advancements are broadening our understanding of the cosmos, and they might have significant repercussions for the future of humanity.

8.2 The Impact of AI and IoT

The Internet of Things (IoT) and Artificial Intelligence (AI) are two of the most game-changing technical developments that have occurred in our time. When combined, they have the ability to revolutionize various areas of our lives, including how we work and live, as well as how industries operate and connect with the world. Specifically, the combination of these two factors has the potential to revolutionize various aspects of our lives. This relationship between AI and IoT is more than just a collaboration in the field of technology; it is also a driver of the Fourth Industrial Revolution.

AI: The Powerhouse Behind the Internet of Things

AI, or artificial intelligence, refers to the capacity of machines and computer systems to imitate human intelligence. This provides the machines with the ability to comprehend, reason, and make choices. Because of this capability, AI is able to derive useful insights from data, identify trends, and even learn from fresh information.

In the context of the Internet of Things (IoT), artificial intelligence plays a crucial role in making sense of the huge amounts of data created by interconnected devices. These gadgets, which can be found anywhere from smart thermostats in homes to sensors in manufacturing plants, gather data on a variety of factors in a continuous manner. AI plays a critical role in the processing and analysis of this data in real time, delivering valuable information and insights that can be put into action.

1. **Improved Capabilities for Analyzing Data and Making Decisions**
   The combination of artificial intelligence and the internet of things produces stronger data analytics and decision-making skills. The data collected by Internet of Things devices can be analyzed by AI algorithms, which can then find trends and make predictions based on that data. For example, Internet of Things (IoT) sensors can monitor soil moisture and crop health in agriculture. At the same time, artificial intelligence (AI) algorithms can forecast ideal irrigation schedules and spot diseases early on, which leads to greater crop yields and better management of resources.
2. **Automated Real-Time Responses and Processes**
   Processing and analysis of data in real time, as provided by AI and the Internet of Things, enables rapid response to changing situations. In the business

world, Internet of Things (IoT) sensors installed in machinery can offer data on performance and wear, and artificial intelligence systems can make decisions on maintenance in real time, which can reduce downtime and increase efficiency. In a similar vein, artificial intelligence can be used in smart cities to evaluate traffic data collected by Internet of Things (IoT) sensors in order to improve the timing of traffic signals, hence reducing congestion and shortening travel times.

3. **An Increased Focus on the Individual**
   AI and IoT are enabling a level of personalisation that has never been seen before, which is altering the experience that customers have. IoT devices powered by AI, for instance, can monitor the preferences and actions of customers in the retail sector, allowing for the customization of product recommendations and marketing campaigns. Wearable Internet of Things devices can improve patient care and wellness by monitoring vital signs and delivering personalized health recommendations based on AI analysis. These capabilities are useful in the field of healthcare.
4. **Maintenance that is Predictive**

Predictive maintenance is one of the most significant effects brought about by the combination of AI and the Internet of Things. IoT sensors are able to detect early indicators of wear or malfunctions in machines, vehicles, or infrastructure since they continuously monitor the performance and condition of these things. Artificial intelligence may then examine this data to determine when maintenance is required, so avoiding expensive breakdowns and lowering the cost of maintenance.

Internet of Things: Giving AI More Eyes and Ears

The term "Internet of Things" refers to a network of connected devices and physical items that are able to collect and share data with one another. These devices may contain sensors, cameras, and other types of apparatus that are outfitted with communication capabilities. These capabilities enable the devices to send data to centralized servers or to other types of apparatus.

In the context of artificial intelligence (AI), the internet of things provides the data sources that are necessary for AI algorithms to work properly. IoT devices serve as the "eyes and ears" of AI systems, continually providing these systems with data from the actual world. This data is critical for generating well-informed choices and performing appropriate actions.

1. **High-Tech Dwellings and Urban Areas**
   In smart homes, Internet of Things (IoT) gadgets like smart thermostats, security cameras, and voice assistants collect data on the temperature, the level of security, and the user's individual preferences. Artificial intelligence processes this data to maximize efficiency in energy use, improve safety, and provide ease. IoT sensors in smart cities collect data on air quality, traffic, and energy usage,

which enables artificial intelligence to make informed judgments regarding the management of traffic, the collection of waste, and the distribution of energy.

2. **Health care services**
   Wearable fitness trackers, remote patient monitoring systems, and even ingestible sensors are examples of the types of IoT devices used in the healthcare industry. These gadgets send information on vital signs, physical activity, and medication compliance to medical professionals about their patients. After that, AI can analyze this data to monitor patient health and provide early warning signals or recommendations for individualized treatment.
3. **Applications in the Industrial Sector**
   IoT sensors in manufacturing machines, logistics, and supply chains collect data regarding product quality, as well as performance metrics such as temperature and humidity, in commercial and industrial settings. Artificial intelligence can examine this data to anticipate faults in equipment, improve production processes, and guarantee product quality.
4. **Keeping an Eye on the Environment**

Environmental sensors that are enabled with the internet of things collect data on the air and water quality, as well as the weather conditions and the health of the soil. The use of AI to analyze this data allows for the monitoring of environmental changes, the prediction of natural disasters, and the informing of decisions about public policy.

Synergy, or the Process of Changing Industries

In the manufacturing industry, predictive maintenance, quality control, and process optimization are helping to increase productivity while simultaneously decreasing unplanned downtime.

In the field of healthcare, improvements in patient outcomes are being driven by remote patient monitoring, earlier disease detection, and more individualized treatment suggestions.

Agriculture: Improvements in agricultural yields and long-term viability are being made thanks to increased use of precision farming techniques and more efficient use of available resources.

Smart grids and demand forecasting are helping to improve energy distribution while simultaneously reducing overall energy waste.

Transportation is undergoing a paradigm shift as a result of the introduction of autonomous vehicles, improved traffic flow, and predictive maintenance.

Retail is benefiting from increased sales and increased customer happiness thanks to improvements in inventory management, consumer analytics, and personalized marketing.

Concerns and Things to Take Into Account

The combination of AI with IoT poses a number of obstacles and things to think about, despite the fact that it has enormous potential.

Privacy and Security: The vast amount of data processed by AI and generated by IoT devices presents substantial privacy and security concerns due to the volume of data collected. It is of the utmost importance to both protect data and guarantee the secure transfer of information.

Realizing the full potential of AI-IoT systems requires ensuring interoperability, which means ensuring that different platforms and devices for the internet of things can function together without a hitch.

Regulation: Governments and regulatory agencies are struggling to determine how to manage the ethical and legal implications of AI and IoT, particularly in reference to the acquisition, utilization, and accountability of data.

Scalability: As the number of Internet of Things devices continues to increase at an exponential rate, scalability challenges will need to be solved in order to manage the vast influx of data and the processing demands of AI.

The impact of the cooperation between AI and IoT is not restricted to the realm of technology; rather, it represents a revolution in society. It is affecting how we work, how we live, and how we engage with the rest of the world. As these technologies continue to develop and mature, their combined power will impact the future. They will offer novel answers to problems that have persisted for a long time and create new opportunities across a variety of industries. The transformative combination of AI and IoT has the potential to make the world smarter, more efficient, and more connected. This potential cannot be denied, despite the fact that the path will not be without obstacles.

8.3 Ethical Considerations in a Hyper-Connected World

Ethical considerations are more important than they have ever been in our hyper-connected world, as the lines between the digital and physical worlds continue to blur. As technology becomes increasingly intertwined with every aspect of our lives, from our personal relationships to the operations of our businesses, we are forced to wrestle with significant moral concerns in order to ensure that technological advancement does not come at the expense of ethical ideals and the well-being of individuals.

Concerns Regarding Privacy:

In today's hyper-connected society, one of the most serious issues from an ethical standpoint is the collecting and exploitation of individuals' personal data. There is a potential for people' privacy to be compromised as a result of the widespread adoption of data-driven analytics, social media platforms, and Internet of Things (IoT) devices. Companies have a need for data in order to improve their services, but they also have a responsibility to protect their customers' privacy. The gathering and utilization of data should be guided by ethical norms, such as informed permission and methods that are transparent with the data.

Concerning Unfairness and Bias in Algorithms:

Decision-making processes in fields such as employment, lending, and criminal justice are rapidly being influenced by machine learning and AI systems. On the other hand, these algorithms have the potential to continue the prejudice and bias that was present in the training data. It is of the utmost importance from a moral standpoint to check that algorithms are fair. In order to accomplish this, it is necessary to eliminate bias in the training data, implement transparent algorithms, and establish explicit accountability when prejudice is discovered.

Inclusion in the Digital Age:

As the global community grows more interconnected, it is imperative that we think about individuals who may be left behind. It is of the utmost importance to ensure that the benefits of technology are available to all individuals, regardless of their social standing, location, or physical capabilities, as this poses a significant ethical challenge. In order to advance digital equity, it is vital to make efforts to close the digital divide, make internet access more inexpensive, and create digital interfaces that are accessible to all users.

Protecting Information and Preventing Cyberattacks:

Cybersecurity and data protection are of the utmost importance when it comes to ethical considerations in a world where private, financial, and other sensitive information is increasingly held online. It is not only important for individuals' personal privacy, but also for the nation's overall security, to make certain that digital systems are safe and resistant to cyberattacks.

Influence on the Environment:

A considerable negative effect on the environment is being caused by the expansion of data centers and linked gadgets. Ethical considerations relating to sustainability and environmental responsibility require both individuals and corporations to lessen their digital carbon footprints in order to act responsibly toward the environment. Ethical remedies to these problems include the development of green technologies and data centers that use less energy.

Addiction to Digital Devices and One's Health:

There is a correlation between hyperconnectivity and digital addiction, which can have a severe impact on mental and emotional health. Ethical considerations include the creation of technologies that encourage healthy usage, the prevention of children's addiction to screen time, and the promotion of responsible digital citizenship.

Disinformation and Manipulation Through Digital Means:

The proliferation of erroneous information, the creation of "deep fakes," and other forms of online manipulation provide a moral challenge to the integrity of information and the operation of democratic societies. It is imperative that individuals, social media platforms, and governments all shoulder their fair share of the responsibility for combating misinformation and fostering media literacy.

Taking Responsibilities and Being Accountable:

An ongoing discussion centers on who should be held accountable for the ethical repercussions that come with having hyper-connected systems. Companies in the technology sector, governmental organizations, and individual users each bear some of the duty for ethical issues.

In order to maintain openness and proper supervision, clear lines of accountability need to be created.

Finding a Middle Ground Between Convenience and Ethical Values:

While increased connection improves convenience, it also has the potential to muddy the distinctions between right and wrong. For example, the use of facial recognition technology in public places might make people feel safer, but it might also invade their privacy. The task of finding a happy medium between practical concerns and moral principles is one that never goes away.

In our increasingly interconnected society, it is imperative that ethical considerations drive technology innovation. To ensure that technology serves humanity's best interests and does not compromise our fundamental ethical standards, it is the obligation of individuals, organizations, and legislators to ensure that technology does not violate these ideals. We will only be able to fully exploit the possibilities of a hyper-connected world by addressing these ethical problems. In doing so, we will also be able to maintain our fundamental values and ideals.

8.4 Speculations on 6G and Beyond

It is only normal for us to be curious about the future at this juncture, given that we are on the verge of the 5G technology becoming commonplace. As the world of technology continues to gaze toward the future, anticipation and conjecture over 6G and higher levels of connectivity are already gaining steam. In this section, we take a deeper look into some of the developing ideas and opportunities around these next-generation networks.

1. **Increased Transfer Rates and Decreased Delay Times:**
   The basis for 6G is expected to be set by 5G, and it is anticipated that 6G would deliver even higher data throughput and lower latency than 5G. It is hypothesized that it will achieve rates in the terabits per second (Tbps) region, which will make it possible to communicate in high resolution holograms in real time and facilitate nearly instantaneous data transfers.
2. **Improvements to Connectivity:**
   It is anticipated that 6G will bring connectivity to hitherto unreached and neglected regions. It is possible that satellite-based networks and high-altitude devices, such as stratospheric balloons and drones, could play an important part in the process of providing global coverage.
3. **Communication on the Quantum Level:**
   A fascinating feature of 6G conjecture is the possibility of quantum communication. The use of quantum technology has the potential to offer unrivaled

levels of security as well as the capacity to send information across great distances with virtually no lag time. Quantum key distribution, often known as QKD, is a method that can strengthen encryption and ensure the safety of data transport, making it almost impossible to hack.

4. **Efficient Use of Energy:**
   It is anticipated that 6G networks will have a lower carbon footprint. This is absolutely necessary to address worries about the environment and to lengthen the amount of time that Internet of Things devices may run on their batteries. There is a possibility that sustainable power sources, such as technology for energy collecting and transceivers that are more efficient, will be incorporated into 6G infrastructure.
5. **Incorporation of AI:**
   A significant part in the development of 6G and beyond will be played by artificial intelligence. It will be utilized to improve network management, personalize service delivery, and strengthen security measures. The combination of AI and 6G could result in networks that are intelligent, adaptive, and dynamically responsive to the requirements of users.
6. **Intelligent Spaces and Digital Doppelgänger:**
   It is anticipated that 6G would make it possible to create digital twin worlds that are both immersive and intelligent. Applications in smart cities, industrial automation, and virtual reality could all benefit from the utilization of this technology. It enables a seamless connection to be made between the actual world and the digital world.
7. **Brain-Computer Interfaces:**
   Brain-computer interfaces, also known as BCIs, have the potential to become more widespread with the introduction of 6G, which will make it easier for the human brain to communicate directly with digital equipment. This technology has the potential to completely transform the medical field, the communication industry, and the entertainment industry.
8. **Obstacles Relating to Ethical Considerations and Safety:**
   Concerns of a substantial ethical and security nature are being raised in tandem with the development of 6G. The combination of AI and BCIs brings up concerns around data security, permission, and privacy of user information. It will be of the utmost importance to protect these networks from cyberattacks and ensure that sophisticated technologies are utilized in a responsible manner.
9. **Exploration of Outer Space and Beyond:**
   Space exploration may be greatly aided by the application of 6G forces. It is possible that it might support communication with spacecraft, satellites, and perhaps potential future colonies on celestial worlds like Mars.
10. **Collaboration on Regulatory Matters at the International Level:**

The development of 6G will require cooperation between countries all over the world and the use of defined protocols. To ensure that technology is used in an ethical manner and is secure as well as accessible, regulatory agencies and governments will need to collaborate to create the necessary frameworks.

It is vital to keep in mind that these technologies are still in their infancy; despite the fact that these rumors create an enticing image of the possibilities of 6G and beyond, they are not yet fully developed. The process of putting these ideas into practice will be laden with difficulties, including issues pertaining to technology, regulations, and ethical concerns. However, the potential of 6G and beyond promises an appealing voyage into a future in which connectivity and technology may dramatically transform our environment once again in ways that we can only begin to understand. This future holds great promise.

Chapter 9

The Role of Telecommunications in Society

Telecommunications, also known as the transfer of information over vast distances for the purpose of communication, have evolved to the point where they are now an essential component of modern society. Its influence is widespread and extends to many spheres of human activity, from interpersonal interactions to the management of multinational corporations. This all-encompassing investigation into the function of telecommunications in contemporary society dives into the field's historical development, technological breakthroughs, social ramifications, and future prospects. The findings illustrate the multidimensional impact that telecommunications has had on human interactions, economies, and worldwide connectedness.

The Development of Telecommunications Throughout History

Early methods of communication included the use of smoke signals, drums, and other forms of visual and auditory clues. The history of telecommunications may be traced back to prehistoric times. The development of the telegraph in the 19th century was a big step forward in terms of communication since it made it possible to send messages across extended distances using Morse code. Alexander Graham Bell's invention of the telephone subsequently brought about a revolution in the field of communication by making it possible to have voice discussions in real time. This innovation was crucial in laying the groundwork for today's sophisticated communications networks.

The Development of the Internet and Other Forms of Electronic Communication

The second part of the 20th century witnessed the emergence of digital communication technology, which eventually led to the invention of the internet, a force that has had a significant transformative impact on contemporary society. The manner in which people and businesses communicated underwent a sea change after the advent of electronic mail (email), instant messaging (IM), and platforms for social media (social media platforms). The rapid growth of the internet has made it easier to exchange information on a worldwide scale, which has contributed to the development of a more linked global community.

Infrastructure and Technologies of the Telecommunications Industry

The infrastructure of telecommunications is made up of a complicated network of cables, satellites, and wireless technologies that allow for the transmission of data and communication over extremely great distances. The use of fiber optic cables has become a fundamental component of high-speed internet connectivity because of their ability to ensure the uninterrupted movement of significant amounts of data. Additionally, developments in wireless technology such as 4G and 5G have changed mobile communication, providing consumers with unparalleled connectivity and access to information. This empowers individuals to do more with their mobile devices.

Influence on the Connectivity and Economies of the World

The development of telecommunications has been an essential factor in the improvement of global connection, which has made it possible for businesses to expand their activities beyond the confines of certain locations. Trade, banking, and business on a global scale are extremely dependent on the effectiveness of communication and data interchange provided by telecommunications networks. The capacity to hold video conferences, virtual meetings, and real-time data transfers has made it easier for multinational firms and worldwide supply chains to flourish, which in turn has fostered economic interdependence among different nations.

The Effects of Communication Technologies on Society

The broad adoption of telecommunications technology has had significant societal repercussions, affecting the way in which individuals communicate with one another, access information, and engage with the communities in which they live. Platforms for social media have fundamentally altered the ways in which individuals initiate and sustain connections, exchange experiences, and participate in online communities. Additionally, the advent of modern communications technologies has made it possible to democratize information and provided individuals with access to a wider range of knowledge and points of view.

The Education and Communications Industries

The development of distance learning and other forms of online education has been made possible by technological advances in telecommunications. Students all over the world now have access to more educational possibilities thanks to the rise of online educational platforms, virtual classrooms, and interactive learning tools. These innovations have overcome geographical barriers and made it possible for students to receive a quality education regardless of where they live. In addition, the development of telecommunications has made possible the conducting of joint research and the exchange of knowledge among academics and researchers located all over the world.

Both the Medical Field and the Telecommunications Industry

Telemedicine and other forms of remote patient monitoring are two areas in which the healthcare industry has reaped considerable benefits from developments in communications technology. Individuals who live in underserved or rural areas now have improved access to medical consultations, diagnoses, and treatment suggestions thanks to technological advancements in the field of telecommunications that have made it easier to conduct these procedures over the internet. The combination of telecommunications systems and medical equipment has made it possible to monitor and analyze patient data in real time, which has resulted in better patient outcomes and more individualized approaches to healthcare.

The Effects of Communications Technology on Culture

The spread of cultural content such as literature, music, films, and art has been made easier because to the development of telecommunications technology, which has broken down geographical barriers and encouraged cultural interaction. Digital platforms have enabled artists, musicians, and content providers to reach audiences all over the world, which has contributed to the promotion of cultural diversity and the development of an understanding between different cultures. Despite this, concerns over the homogeneity of culture and the preservation of cultural legacy in the age of digital technology continue to exist.

Confrontations, as well as Ethical Considerations

The growing adoption of various forms of communication technology has ushered in a host of new problems and ethical questions for society to ponder. In this day and age of digital technology, issues pertaining to privacy, data security, and the moral use of personal information have become of the utmost importance. Questions pertaining to data ownership, permission, and transparency have been brought to light as a result of the collecting and exploitation of big data for commercial purposes. In addition, the digital divide, which refers to differences in access to various forms of information and communication technology, has brought to light the requirement for inclusive and equitable digital infrastructure.

Cybersecurity and Information and Communication Technology

The growing interconnection of telecommunications networks has led to an increase in the dangers associated with cybersecurity. As a result, data breaches, cyber-attacks, and the theft of information have become serious concerns for individuals, corporations, and governments. The protection of sensitive information, the prevention of illegal access, and the creation of effective cybersecurity protocols have become necessities for the preservation of trust in telecommunications networks and digital infrastructure.

Future Innovations and Trends in the Industry

Further technological advancement and revolutionary advancements are likely to be a part of the telecoms industry's future. The introduction of 5G networks promises data speeds that have never been seen before, low latency, and improved connectivity, which will revolutionize the way in which individuals and organizations communicate with one another and conduct their daily operations. Additionally, developments in artificial intelligence, the Internet of Things (IoT), and blockchain technology are anticipated to transform the landscape of the telecommunications industry, which will result in the development of a digital ecosystem that is more connected, safe, and intelligent.

The field of telecommunications has developed into an essential component of modern society, having an impact on the ways in which individuals communicate with one another, do business, have access to information, and take part in worldwide networks. The historical development of it, the technological advances that it has brought about, and the sociological ramifications that it has had have all contributed to the formation of the contemporary world, making global connectivity, economic growth, and cultural exchange more possible. The potential of telecommunications to stimulate innovation, interconnectedness, and the growth of society is unrivaled despite the fact that technology continues to create problems and ethical considerations. The world as a whole will likely continue to embrace digital transformation, which will cause the role of telecommunications in society to continue to expand. This will have a significant impact on the future of human contact and global connectedness.

9.1 Social and Economic Impacts

The broad adoption of technologies related to communications has had significant effects, both socially and economically, on societies all over the world. The transmission of information and communication over great distances is included in the field of telecommunications, which has radically revolutionized the way in which people interact with one another, gain access to information, do business, and connect with people in other parts of the world. In this investigation, we look into the social and economic implications of telecommunications, with a particular emphasis on the ways in which technology has helped to bridge gaps, provided possibilities, and faced obstacles in today's interconnected world.

The Influence of Telecommunications on the Economy

Connectivity and Trade on a Global Scale:

The expansion of global connectivity as well as the volume of international trade has been significantly aided by technological advances. It has become more simpler for companies to interact and collaborate with clients and partners located in different parts of the world. Travel expenses have been greatly cut because to advancements in teleconferencing and digital communication, which have also made it possible for global firms to broaden their scope.

E-commerce and Business Conducted Online:

The development of telecommunications has directly contributed to the expansion of e-commerce and online business. Global marketplaces have been created by companies such as Amazon, Alibaba, and eBay through the utilization of the internet and various telecommunications networks. Additionally, small and medium-sized enterprises have profited from this development because they are now able to more easily access customers in different parts of the world.

The Digitization of Everything:

The proliferation of telecommunications services has been a driving force behind the digital transformation of various businesses. It has enabled businesses to simplify their operations, collect and analyze data, and enhance the experiences they provide for their customers. The widespread use of cloud computing, the internet of things (IoT), and big data analytics are only now becoming feasible thanks to the proliferation of high-speed internet and dependable telecommunications networks.

Creating New Jobs:

In a number of different ways, the field of telecommunications has helped to spur the creation of new jobs. It has given birth to entire sectors, such as the creation of mobile applications and data security. Additionally, the capability of working remotely, which has been made possible by advancements in telecommunications, has made employment prospects available to individuals who may not live in close proximity to traditional job hubs.

Innovation and entrepreneurial endeavors:

The proliferation of modern communication technologies has made it easier for entrepreneurs and innovators to launch new businesses. These days, new businesses can connect with customers all over the world and work together with partners from all over the world. The strength of telecommunications can be directly related to the growth of tech centres in places such as Silicon Valley, Tel Aviv, and Shenzhen. These cities include Shenzhen.

The Effects of Telecommunications on Society

Communication on a Global Scale:

The development of telecommunications has enabled people to contact with their loved ones and friends located in other parts of the world, bridging the gap that previously existed between them. Because of this, social relationships have been enhanced, and the world has become a smaller and more interconnected place. Video conversations and various forms of social media have rapidly become indispensable communication tools for long-distance partnerships.

Education & Learning Throughout One's Life:

Education has been revolutionized by technological advances like the internet and telecommunications. Education has become more available as a result of the proliferation of e-learning platforms and online classes. Students now have access to a wide variety of materials and experts regardless of their location. In times of disaster, such as the COVID-19 epidemic, communications technology has also made it possible to learn remotely from a distance.

Access to Medical Care:

The field of medicine has been profoundly altered by the introduction of telecommunications. Patients now have the ability to consult with their healthcare doctors via telemedicine and telehealth services, which eliminates the need for patients to physically travel. People living in underserved or rural areas stand to benefit the most from this development.

Movements of the People and Political Activism:

The proliferation of telecommunications has made social movements and activism more accessible. Platforms for social media have been utilized to organize demonstrations, increase awareness about social concerns, and hold those in power accountable for their actions. The power of telecommunications has been utilized for the purpose of bringing about social change by movements such as the Arab Spring and #BlackLivesMatter.

Intercultural Communication and the Consumption of Media:

The advancement of telecommunications has made it possible for people all over the world to share their cultures and consume media from other regions. People have been exposed to a wider variety of cultures and points of view as a result of the proliferation of streaming services, digital newspapers, and internet information. It has also resulted in the proliferation of pop cultural phenomena and the formation of fan communities all over the world.

Inequalities and Obstacles in the Way

The "Digital Divide":

The term "digital divide" refers to the disparity that exists between people who have access to contemporary forms of communication and digital technology and those who do not. This divide may be caused by factors such as location, income, or inadequate infrastructure. The digital divide still presents a serious barrier that must be overcome.

Confidentiality and safety:

Concerns concerning data privacy and cybersecurity have been brought to the forefront as a result of society's growing reliance on telecommunications. Recent headline-grabbing problems include data breaches, stolen identities, and widespread spying. The challenges of keeping personal information secure and preventing breaches in the security of telecommunications networks are never-ending.

Incorrect information and deliberately false information:

Due to the ease with which information can be disseminated because to advancements in telecommunications, it is also possible for incorrect information and disinformation to proliferate rapidly. The dissemination of false information and hoaxes over the internet can have real-world repercussions, including an impact on public perception, political discourse, and even public health.

Isolation from Other People:

Despite the fact that telecommunications have brought individuals from all over the world closer together, there has been an increase in worries around social isolation. Particularly among younger generations, over use of digital communication can lead to a reduction in face-to-face encounters as well as feelings of isolation.

Displacement from One's Job:

Although the development of telecommunications has led to the creation of new work opportunities, it has also resulted in the loss of jobs in particular fields. The demand for certain forms of labor has decreased as a result of automation and digital transformation, particularly in manufacturing and occupations that involve regular administrative responsibilities.

The Prospects for the Field of Telecommunications

In the years to come, we can expect to see a further development in the function that telecommunications play in our society. It is to be anticipated that as the globe goes toward 5G and beyond, data speeds will accelerate even further, latency will decrease, and greater connectedness will be achieved. Integration of emerging technologies such as blockchain, artificial intelligence, and the Internet of Things (IoT) will continue to influence the economic and social environment in the future.

9.2 Ethical and Cultural Implications

The pervasive nature of telecommunications in our everyday lives has resulted in a wide variety of ethical and cultural ramifications being pushed to the fore. We need to be able to negotiate the complicated environment of ethical issues and cultural shifts in order to participate in digital dialogues, share our lives on social media, and utilize technology for both personal and professional reasons. In this investigation, we look into the ethical and cultural implications of telecommunications, underlining the challenges and opportunities they provide in the ever-evolving digital world in which we live.

Implications for Ethical Behavior

Privacy and the Protection of Data:

Ethical questions are raised when it comes to the gathering, storing, and using of an individual's personal data in the digital arena. Companies that deal in telecommunications and digital platforms collect large amounts of information about their users, which might range from surfing habits to location data. Important ethical imperatives include the appropriate treatment of this data, the protection of user privacy, and the prevention of data breaches. Users should be able to exercise control over their own data and comprehend what is being done with it.

The Relationship Between Surveillance and Civil Liberties:

Concerns about the potential for civil liberties to be infringed upon as a result of government

surveillance have been sparked by the ease with which we can now communicate with one another. A crucial ethical problem is striking a balance between protecting national security and protecting the privacy of individuals. It is incumbent upon governments to ensure that the surveillance mechanisms they put in place are proportionate, legal, and respectful of the rights of the people under their watch.

Incorrect information and deliberately false information:

Concerns concerning the ease with which false information and disinformation can be disseminated because to advancements in telecommunications technology have recently come to the forefront. Important factors to take into account include the ethical obligation that information makers, platforms, and individuals have to distribute information that is true and truthful. In this day and age, being able to evaluate facts, analyze critically, and be media literate are all extremely important abilities.

The Information Gap and Other Inequalities:

An ethical problem is posed by the digital gap, which can be defined as differences in access to various forms of electronic communication technology.

It is necessary to find a way to bridge this divide in order to ensure that all people have equal opportunity to access information, educational possibilities, and economic prospects. Companies in the telecommunications industry, national governments, and international organizations all need to collaborate on making internet access more fair.

Substance Use Disorder and Mental Health :

Because of the addictive nature of digital platforms, particularly social media, ethical problems have been raised. There is a risk to users' mental health when applications are purposefully designed to attract and maintain their attention. It is an ethical responsibility to make certain that new technology is developed with the health and safety of its users in mind.

Repercussions for the culture

Globalization and the Spread of Different Cultures:

An unprecedented level of cultural interchange has been made possible because to advances in communication technology. Interactions between people of different cultures allow for the exchange of traditions and the cultivation of an appreciation for alternative points of view. However, this globalization also raises worries regarding the potential loss of cultural diversity as well as the potential for the homogenization of different civilizations.

Communities and Identities in Cyberspace:

Communities and subcultures have emerged online as a result of the proliferation of telecommunications and the internet. The same interests, hobbies, or identities that bring these communities together are frequently at the center of their activities. They have the potential to provide individuals with the sense of support and belonging that they may not be able to find in their immediate physical environment.

Movements of the People and Political Activism:

The proliferation of communication technologies has facilitated the growth of social movements and activism. Platforms for social media have played an essential role in the organization of protests, the raising of awareness about societal issues, and the holding of those in power accountable. The power of telecommunications has been utilized for the purpose of bringing about social change by movements such as #MeToo and #BlackLivesMatter.

Communication and the Use of Language:

Language and communication have both been affected by the rise of the internet. People who come from a variety of linguistic backgrounds communicate with one another using a common language, which is most typically English.

In addition, the use of emojis, memes, and online lingo has resulted in the creation of new forms of digital communication that are not limited by linguistic constraints.

The Digital Divide and Efforts to Increase Inclusion:

The digital gap is a problem not only from a cultural but also from an ethical standpoint. It is essential to have access to telecommunications and the internet in order to maintain cultural traditions and to express oneself. It is possible to share and celebrate indigenous arts, languages, and customs through the use of digital means; however, this is only possible if fair access is maintained.

The Confluence of Ethical Principles and Cultural Values

The dissemination of cultural content through telecommunications platforms, such as music, films, and literature, can give rise to ethical considerations around intellectual property, piracy, and appropriate pay for artists and creators of the cultural content.

The communities and subcultures that develop online and in digital spaces frequently develop their own sets of ethical norms and codes of conduct, which are reflective of the values and interests of the people who make up those communities and subcultures.

Even while it is a method for bringing about cultural and social change, digital activism also brings up ethical problems around the usage of online platforms for the sake of advocacy and protest.

The globalization of culture through the use of telecommunications forces societies to confront the difficulty of striking a balance between the maintenance of their cultural legacy and participation in the global digital environment.

The Prospects for Ethical and Cultural Impacts in the Future

The ramifications of telecommunications on ethics and culture will continue to develop in tandem with the progression of technology and the adaptation of society. New technologies, such as artificial intelligence, augmented reality, and virtual reality, will give rise to new ethical questions about privacy, identification, and the blurring of the line between the digital and physical worlds.

To successfully navigate these ramifications, a multi-pronged strategy will be required. It is necessary for individuals, organizations, and governments to collaborate on the development of ethical frameworks, the protection of personal information, and the upholding of cultural variety by technological systems. In addition, as the digital change of society continues, the importance of media literacy and digital education will only grow.

9.3 Environmental Sustainability

The idea of environmental sustainability has emerged as a crucial factor in the telecommunications business in this age of rapid digital innovation and interconnected communication. This is because of the interrelated nature of modern communication. In spite of the fact that the revolutionary force of telecommunications has transformed the way in which we connect with one another and engage with one another, it has also brought to the forefront the environmental concerns related with energy consumption, technological waste, and the carbon footprint of digital infrastructure. In this investigation, we delve into the environmental consequences of telecommunications and highlight the industry's efforts toward sustainability as well as the plans for building a greener digital future. In addition, we look at some of the potential solutions to these environmental issues.

Consumption of Energy and Relative Carbon Footprint

The Demand for Energy and Data Centers:

The growth of data centers, which are necessary for the storage and processing of enormous amounts of digital information, has resulted in a huge increase in the quantity of energy that is consumed. These data centers have an ongoing need for maintenance and cooling, which results in significant amounts of carbon emissions. It is absolutely necessary to implement green data center practices in addition to using energy-efficient cooling systems and renewable energy sources in order to lessen the negative impact that data centers have on the surrounding environment.

Infrastructure of the Network as Well as Connectivity:

The proliferation of telecommunications networks, particularly the introduction of 4G and 5G technologies, has contributed to an increase in the demand for infrastructure that requires a significant amount of energy. The use of considerable amounts of energy by base stations, cell towers, and other network equipment is one factor that contributes to the overall carbon footprint of the sector. The environmental effect of network infrastructure can be reduced by incorporating renewable energy sources, optimizing transmission technologies, and implementing energy-efficient network designs.

The Management of Electronic Waste

Lifespan of a Device and Generation of Electronic Waste:

A rise in the amount of electronic garbage, sometimes known as "e-waste," has been attributed to the rapid production of electronic gadgets such as smartphones, tablets, and network equipment. Eliminating waste in an appropriate manner and recycling old electronics are both necessary steps in the fight against the release of harmful substances into the atmosphere. The implementation of sustainable product design, the promotion of device longevity, and the establishment of programs for the management of electronic waste are essential elements in the process of reducing the negative impact that telecommunications hardware has on the environment.

Sustainable Business Practices and the Circular Economy:

It is possible to dramatically reduce the environmental impact of telecommunications technology by making the transition to a form of economy known as the circular economy. In this model, resources are reused, recycled, and repurposed. In order for manufacturers to assure the proper disposal and recycling of products, they can use environmentally friendly materials, design their products to be easily repaired and upgraded, and set up take-back programs.

Integration of Renewable Energy Sources

Implementation of Solar and Wind Power:

It is possible for the carbon footprint of telecommunications operations to be greatly reduced with the implementation of renewable energy sources such as solar and wind power. Effective ways for shifting towards a more sustainable energy mix include investing in on-site solar installations, sourcing energy from wind farms, and entering into power purchase agreements with providers of renewable energy.

Designing for Energy Efficiency in Infrastructure:

Furthering the cause of environmental sustainability can be accomplished through the planning and development of energy-efficient telecommunications infrastructure. It is possible to cut energy consumption and operational expenses while simultaneously minimizing the industry's impact on the environment by putting into practice environmentally friendly building techniques, such as optimizing the use of natural light and implementing energy management systems.

Practices That Are Sustainable Within the Supply Chain

A Responsible Approach to Sourcing and Managing Materials:

It is essential, in order to lessen the negative effects that supply chains for telecommunications have on the environment, to promote sustainable mining methods and ensure that raw materials are sourced in a responsible manner. It is possible to develop a supply chain that is more sustainable and cognizant of its impact on the environment by implementing transparency and traceability measures, adhering to ethical labor norms, and limiting the use of hazardous materials in device manufacturing.

Green Partnerships and Sourcing and Ethical Purchasing:

It is possible to foster sustainable practices all throughout the telecommunications business by engaging in environmentally friendly procurement methods. These activities include selecting vendors and suppliers with strong environmental credentials. For the purpose of developing a greener and more sustainable supply chain ecosystem, the establishment of ethical alliances, the promotion of sustainable innovation, and the prioritization of environmentally friendly products and services are all vital components.

Education and Sensitization of the Public

Education of Customers and Acceptance of Responsibilities:

It is possible to encourage responsible usage and sustainable behaviors by educating consumers about the environmental impact of telecommunications and raising their knowledge of this impact. Users can be empowered to make environmentally responsible choices in their digital lifestyles by being educated about energy-efficient device usage, e-waste recycling programs, and the benefits of adopting renewable energy sources through the dissemination of information about these topics.

Responsibility of Corporations Towards Their Social and Natural Environments:

Within the telecommunications business, embracing programs for corporate social responsibility and pushing for environmentally sustainable practices can be effective ways to achieve positive change. It is possible to demonstrate a commitment to building a greener digital future by providing financial support to environmental advocacy groups, making investments in environmentally responsible research and development, and providing transparent reporting on environmental performance.

Collaboration within the Industry and Support for Advocacy of Policies

Initiatives of Collaboration in Support of Sustainability:

Fostering collective efforts toward environmental sustainability in the telecommunications business can be facilitated by the cultivation of collaborative relationships with industry peers, environmental NGOs, and regulatory agencies. It is possible to speed up the process of transforming the telecommunications business into one that is less harmful to the environment by taking part in industry-wide sustainability efforts, exchanging information about successful practices, and pushing innovation through joint research and development.

Advocacy of Policies and Compliance with Regulations:

It is essential, for the purpose of bringing about systemic change, to advocate for environmental laws and regulatory frameworks that promote sustainability and energy efficiency. It is possible to guarantee that the telecommunications business is in alignment with global efforts to reduce climate change and environmental degradation through engaging with legislators, supporting requirements for environmentally sustainable technologies, and complying with environmental legislation.

9.4 Telecommunications and Human Progress

There is no denying the importance of the role that communications technology plays in human advancement. The development of telecommunications over the past century has brought about profound changes in people's abilities to communicate, gain access to information, run businesses, and engage with the wider world. It has helped drive invention, supported economic growth, spanned geographical divisions, and contributed to many improvements in a wide variety of sectors, among other benefits. In this investigation, we dig into the enormous impact that telecommunications have had on the progression of humankind by highlighting its influence on society, the economy, education, healthcare, and other areas.

Developments in Human Society

Connectivity on a Global Scale:

People living in distant parts of the world are now able to communicate with one another in real time because to advancements in communication and networking technologies. Families that are geographically separated, friends who live in other countries, and coworkers who observe different time zones can all easily converse with one another. Our social networks have grown as a result of our increased interconnection, which has also facilitated the exchange of cultural ideas and contributed to the development of a feeling of global community.

Communication in a Time of Crisis:

The use of telecommunications is critically important in both crisis management and disaster relief efforts. It makes it easier for those who are affected by an emergency to communicate with first responders during situations such as natural disasters, pandemics, or other types of crises. The broadcast of vital information, the coordination of relief operations, and the announcement of important public safety information are all made possible through telecommunications.

Participation in Politics and Political Activism:

Citizens now have the ability to participate in political activity and advocacy because to advancements in telecommunications. Platforms for political dialogue, organizing protests, and raising awareness about social and political concerns have emerged as a result of the proliferation of social media platforms. The Arab Spring, Occupy Wall Street, and the #MeToo movement are all examples of how the rise of telecommunications has contributed to the acceleration of societal shifts.

Innovation and the Promotion of Economic Growth

Operations of Businesses on a Global Scale:

The development of telecommunications has made it possible for companies to compete on a worldwide basis. The ability of multinational firms to connect with their subsidiaries and business partners located all over the world encourages the growth of international commerce and economic interdependence. Additionally, it has made business ownership more accessible to a wider range of people by opening up international markets to start-ups and smaller companies.

Electronic trade and the emerging digital economy:

The development of telecommunications has directly contributed to the expansion of online commercial activity. The power of the internet has been harnessed by online retail platforms such as Amazon, Alibaba, and eBay to establish worldwide marketplaces for buyers and sellers. The retail sector is in the process of being remade as a direct result of advancements in telecommunications, which have caused consumers' shopping, payment, and interaction with businesses to change radically.

Collaboration in the Fields of Innovation and Research:

The increased availability of telecommunications has made it easier for academics and inventors to work together. The sharing of information, the results of research, and the undertaking of joint initiatives across international borders has resulted in significant advancements in the fields of science, technology, and medicine. Telecommunications have been a driving force behind innovations ranging from the Large Hadron Collider to the investigation of worldwide vaccines.

Education and Continued Professional Development

Learning at a Distance and Online Learning:

The use of telecommunications has completely changed the educational system. Students are now able to access courses, resources, and expertise from any location thanks to advancements in distance learning and online learning platforms. This has made education more accessible. The COVID-19 epidemic sped up the acceptance of remote learning, bringing to light the significance of communications technology in the educational setting.

Access to a Variety of Educational Materials:

Access to a wider variety of educational resources has been made possible by advances in communications technology. People from every corner of the globe can now have access to resources such as libraries, research databases, and online classes. Regardless of where an individual lives, they are able to pursue education throughout their lives, engage in learning that is self-directed, access academic materials, and discover new things.

Healthcare and Remote Medical Consultations

The Benefits of Telemedicine and Remote Care:

The delivery of healthcare has been revolutionized by telecommunications. Patients are now able to consult with their healthcare doctors via telemedicine and remote patient monitoring, which has eliminated the need for patients to physically travel to the providers' offices. Individuals who live in underserved or distant areas can especially benefit from receiving care remotely, as this increases their access to medical services.

Sharing and Working Together on Medical Information:

Telecommunications have made it easier for medical personnel to work together and share information with one another, which is beneficial to patient care. Patient care, research, and medical innovation have all been improved as a result of the use of electronic health records (EHRs), telehealth consultations, and telepathology.

Globalization and the Spread of Different Cultures

Interactions Between Cultures:

An unprecedented level of cultural interchange has been made possible because to advances in communication technology. Interactions between people of different cultures allow for the exchange of traditions and the cultivation of an appreciation for alternative points of view. The internet and other forms of digital media have enabled cultural content to travel across geographical boundaries thanks to its widespread availability.

Communication and the Use of Language:

Language and communication have been significantly altered as a result of technological advances such as the internet and telecommunications. People who come from a variety of linguistic backgrounds communicate with one another using a common language, which is most typically English. In addition, the use of emojis, memes, and online lingo has resulted in the creation of new forms of digital communication that are not limited by linguistic constraints.

Sustainability in Relation to the Environment

Sensitivity to the Environment:

The advancement of communications technology is a significant contributor to increased ecological sensitivity. It makes it possible to collect data in real time, monitor the environment remotely, and disseminate information on things like climate change, conservation, and environmentally responsible practices. In order to advocate for the conservation of the environment, environmental organizations and activists use many forms of communication technology.

Working from home and reducing your carbon footprint:

The carbon footprints left behind by commuters and office buildings could be lessened because to advancements in telecommunications technology. The ability to work from home, made possible by advances in telecommunications, has the potential to cut down on emissions of greenhouse gases and reduce the load placed on metropolitan infrastructure.

Concerns and Things to Take Into Account

While advancements in telecommunications have in many respects been a driving force behind human progress, they also create obstacles and warrant scrutiny.

The "digital divide" refers to the disparities in access to telecommunications technologies that continue to exist. This divide is caused by constraints in infrastructure, as well as differences in geography and income. It is necessary to find a way to bridge this divide in order to ensure that all people have equal opportunity to access information, educational possibilities, and economic prospects.

Concerns concerning data privacy and computer security have been brought to the forefront as a result of the rapid development of technology related to telecommunications. Recent headline-grabbing problems include data breaches, stolen identities, and widespread spying. The challenges of securing telecommunications networks and preventing unauthorized access to personally identifiable information are never ending.

Concerns concerning the propagation of false information and disinformation have been brought to the forefront as a direct result of the ease with which information can be disseminated because to advancements in telecommunications. The dissemination of false information and hoaxes over the internet can have real-world repercussions, including an impact on public perception, political discourse, and even public health.

Isolation in Social Relationships Despite the fact that telecommunications have made it possible to connect individuals all over the world, there have also been worries voiced about people being socially isolated. Particularly among younger generations, over use of digital communication can lead to a reduction in face-to-face encounters as well as feelings of isolation.

The Prospects of Human Advancement and Communication Technologies

The future of communications technology provides the potential of even greater connectedness, better data rates, and even more applications that can completely revolutionize our lives. As technological development develops, it will be essential to provide careful attention to issues relating to ethical and equitable access, data security, and responsible usage. To successfully navigate the rapidly changing terrain of the telecommunications business, a holistic approach that includes stakeholders from the government, industry, academic institutions, and civil society will be required.

9 788196 724375

Printed at Repro India Ltd.